For the community, by the community

# Book Project Byte-Sized

*Cloud design principles and architectural recommendations*

**Website:** www.projectbytesized.com

**Twitter:** @ProByteSized

Initiated by

**Christiaan Brinkhoff & Bas van Kaam**

And many others spread across the globe

For the community, by the community



If we printed your name, website, Twitter handle, job role, company name, submission or LinkedIn address incorrectly, we are very sorry. If for whatever reason we forgot to mention your name somewhere, we are even more sorry!

Note, while we initially had placed multiple images in the form of various comics throughout the book, we had to remove them with regard to potential copyright violations. We tried contacting the artists but in most cases we didn't get a reply.



**ISBN:** 9781797692104

**Imprint:** Independently published – Kindle Direct Publishing

2019 1st edition, version 1.0

## Acknowledgements

To all community heroes out there

# THANK

# YOU

A special ***thank you*** goes out to our sponsors: Nutanix, CloudJumper, Goliath, ControlUP, IGEL, Gourami, Parallels, and Salomon IT Solutions.

This book would not have been possible without their help.

# Table of Contents

# First things first

# Foreword

The definition of a foreword according to Wikipedia is:
*"A **foreword** is a (usually short) piece of writing sometimes placed at the beginning of a book or other piece of literature. Typically written by someone other than the primary author of the work, it often tells of some interaction between the writer of the foreword and the book's primary author or the story the book tells."* Makes perfect sense, right?

For obvious reasons, it's unusual for a book author to write his or her own foreword. However, although our names are on the cover, we are the initiators of this wonderful project, not the true authors. This book is written by the community, for the community, and that means all of YOU! That's why in this case it does make sense for us to say a few words before you dig in.

Here goes...

The community is your friend, in more ways than you can think of. Something that Christiaan and Bas experienced throughout the last couple of years. "*It's a special kind of family where everyone is equal and people are treated with respect.*"

While they both started out as junior admins, years ago, they also quickly realized that they found their passion and wanted more – to expand their horizons, so to speak. Of course, back than they didn't know each other.

As they started to learn from others, they thought it would make sense to share what they picked up along the way as well. Through blogs, presentations, webinars, you name it. "*What followed was an amazing roller coaster ride. Luckily, it had (and still has) more ups than downs.*" Even though they *started* at different times in their lives and careers, they both never imagined that it would turn into something as big as it is today.

***"If you can't explain it simply, you don't understand it well enough."*** – Albert Einstein

*"Right from the start, the community, in the broadest sense of the word, was amazing. Supportive in every way, constantly helping each other out, providing honest feedback, and, most importantly, good fun while enjoying a beer (or two)."*

Next, they both started to visit various events around the globe. *"Even though we attended multiple sessions where the presenter was noticeably nervous, we still had, and showed, the deepest respect just for them being up there – and we still do today. It takes guts and hours, or days even, of preparing and getting everything ready. Something you can only admire."*

*"Personally, presenting was a huge step for me. To say that I was scared shitless would be an understatement." According to Bas.* Christiaan didn't seem to have that problem when he started out: he was, or is, more of a *natural* (which has something to do with attending a family BBQ and meeting a guy who asked about what it was that he did for a living – ask Christiaan the next time you run into him). Anyway, Later on Bas decided *enough was enough* and forced himself to attend a presenter clinic and took it from there.

***"Public speaking is like learning to drive and shifting gears in a car. When you know your content, it all goes automatically with adrenaline as engine fuel!"*** – Christiaan Brinkhoff

*"Again, the community was very forgiving and provided honest, but gentle, feedback for me to work with – though the same happened to Christiaan on multiple occasions as well.*

*Having said that, I have to be honest, it's still way beyond my comfort zone, especially when I haven't presented in a while. But hey, that's where the magic happens, right?"* A problem Christiaan doesn't have currently, since he's up in front of thousands throughout the year while visiting various conferences around the world.

Anyway, writing, presenting, sharing material from others, mentoring and educating colleagues and so on, it's all part of the community way of life, and they wouldn't want to have it any other way. *"We're just glad that we are able to give back every once in a while"* – as stated by Bas and Christiaan.

"*The appreciation that comes with it, from all of you guys, the vendors, including the various programs they provide, and others is something we've come to greatly appreciate and love as well."*

***"Do what you love, and you'll never work another day in your life."*** – Marc Anthony

"*With that, we'd like to say thank you for reading, thank you for contributing, and most of all, thank you for your support throughout the years. We have never regretted joining the community and we're looking forward to many more years of great initiatives – cheers!"*

Christiaan and Bas.

## Why this book?

We – *and we'll get to who we are in just a minute* – as community participants know how valuable it can be to share with others what we have learned and picked up during our careers. That's how we all get better, smarter, more effective and efficient at what we do daily. And more importantly, it's fun – we all need a hobby, right?

Throughout the year we spend a great deal of time studying, testing, breaking, and fixing stuff, helping and assisting customers, peers, colleagues, often working late, traveling, attending conferences, webinars, and so on.

It would be a waste to keep it all to ourselves.

That's one of the main reasons why we spend so much time researching, writing, preparing, presenting, and so on. Just to be able to share what we have picked up along the way. It's what we do, like, and love.

Of course, we know the above applies to many of you as well. The amount of community initiatives and information that is freely shared on an almost daily basis is inspiring, to say the least. Not to mention, extremely helpful.

As mentioned in the introduction blog post back in January 2019, the main thought behind this project is to collect as much feedback as possible, potentially helping others.

In the form of Cloud-related design principles, architectural recommendations, tips, tricks, best and/or common practices, helpful and/or funny quotes, you name it. Enabling us to categorize and bundle all the information shared, by the community, for the community – for free! This way we all benefit.

Hopefully, everyone who picked up a copy, either a digital one or the paperback version, will take something useful away from it. But to be honest, we find it very hard to believe this is not the case, given the quality of the content.

We've gone over all submissions one by one and the quality is outstanding: just wait and find out for yourself. We personally know many of the contributors (not all, though) and we can assure you that they are all top-notch professionals *without exception,* with many years of field experience under their belts.

Again, we would like to thank everyone who has contributed to this amazing project. We know how busy you all are and appreciate the time you took out of your schedules.

When we started out, we were aiming for 100+ submissions. What happened next blew our minds, we received a total of 152 submissions. So, there is plenty to go through – we think the end result is something to be very proud of.

Finally, a big thankyou goes out to all who didn't directly contribute but helped spread the word and came up with various suggestions, making this book the success it has turned out to be.

Bas and Christiaan.

## One Laptop per Child – OLPC

As you might have read, we are donating around 2 dollar / euro to the OLPC Foundation for every paperback copy sold.

So, if this is a free digital copy, please consider purchasing a paperback version as well.

Try to think of it like this: you'll own a cool (physical) collector's item, perhaps one with your own name in it, learn about the Cloud in general, and donate to charity! All at the same time.

But seriously, while working on the project we discussed the possibility to donate to charity multiple times. During the first couple of weeks it was mentioned by multiple other community folks as well. At some point we thought, why not?! We're already doing this for free, basically, so why not help those in need as well? That's where our search began.

Since we are in IT we thought it would be nice if the cause in question had anything to do with what we do, on a daily basis. That's how we ended up with 'One Laptop per Child'. Their goal is simple. Well, simple in theory, that is…

***"To empower the children of developing countries to learn by providing one connected laptop to every school-age child."*** – OLPC

Their mission statement, as per their website:

*To create educational opportunities for the world's poorest children by providing each child with a rugged, low-cost, low-power, connected laptop with content and software designed for collaborative, joyful, self-empowered learning.*

When children have access to this type of tools they get engaged in their own education. They learn, share, create, and collaborate. They become connected to each other, to the world and to a brighter future.

More information can be found on their website: www.laptop.org/en

We have purposely raised the list price of the paperback version by 2 dollar / euro give or take, which we will donate to the OLPC Foundation. Again, all costs associated with purchasing a physical copy are purely because of manufacturing costs like paper, ink, manual labor involved, and so on: we do not get any of it.

That's it. Thank you for purchasing or thinking about doing so (and thus donating). Enjoy the book, learn, and have some fun while doing so!

# Numbers and statistics

- We had a total number of 140 contributors from 20 countries, which we think is truly awesome.
- All together this led to 152 submissions.
- Mike Nelson was the very first to the scene. Thank you, Mike, for getting the ball rolling. Many followed shortly after.
- It was also Mike who suggested allowing multiple submissions per person, which we agreed to almost instantly. Something we didn't regret: it got us (and you) some great content.
- Anton van Pelt and Patrick van den Born were the last ones to submit – they submitted together.
- Multiple contributors submitted twice or even more.
- That's also why some submissions go way beyond the maximum of 250 words. Though, once we were a few weeks in we also announced a new max of 500 words, give or take. Some submissions have been bundled as well.
- As mentioned, contributions came in from all over the globe – see the graph on page 16 for an overview.
- Topics ranged from general recommendations, to costs, security, SLAs, technical implementation tips and tricks, and much more. Very diverse. We purposely choose not to disclose the content ***submitted by*** others while the submission window was still open. This way everyone had to do their own thinking not influenced by others, which worked out very nicely.
- We took all submissions and printed them 'as is' with the exception of a couple of minor spelling corrections – these are your thoughts and words, not ours. This is where the guys at ProofProfessor helped us out. It only took them 12 days to go over our manuscript.
- The main font used throughout the book is Arial with a font size of 10. We also used the ITC Officina Sans Std Book font in a size 10 for the quotes in Appendix A, as well as

the **Verdana Pro Black** font in various sizes for most of the quotes throughout the book.

- There are a total of 92 quotes in the book – see appendix A for a complete overview.
- The book consists of **58833 words** in total, which includes all submissions, quotes, names, websites, Twitter handles, LinkedIn addresses, and so on.
- We had 8 fantastic sponsors helping us out: see the accompanying sponsor pages throughout the book.
- It took us about 8 hours per week, per person on average, starting 2 January 2019 to get to the end result you have before you today.
- We were in contact daily, even though we were spread out across the globe from time to time – Christiaan mostly, to be honest.
- We used Slack as our main form of communication, together with some email and WhatsApp.
- We exchanged around 4500 messages throughout the last couple of months, using Slack, that is.
- Google Docs was our friend. We used multiple forms to keep track of who we spoke to (some of you we approached twice: for that we apologize), to write down our ideas and thoughts, we shared a to-do list, and so on. We basically learned as we go – the way we like it best.
- We had a total of 8 face-to-face meetings/lunches to go over things like the inside, the questionnaire, the book cover, the final launch, and more. We both love technology but sometimes it just helps if you can have a chat face to face. We also had multiple Teams/SfB meetings.
- Our project featured on the Citrix MyCUGC community blog page, which was great.
- We *starred* in three podcasts: the Login TechCast, ITProTV, and the Come Get IT podcast.
- We loved every minute of it.

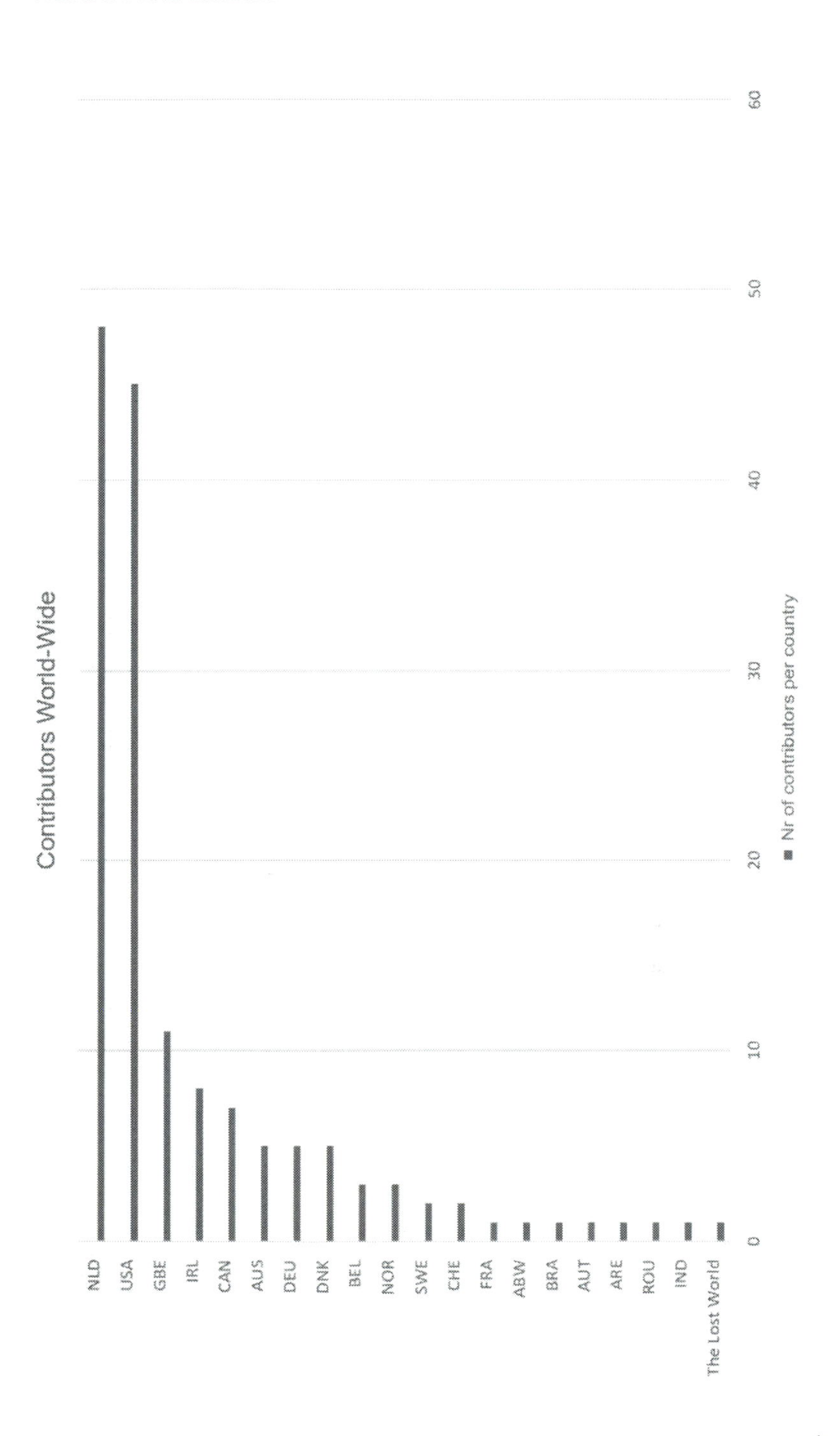
Contributors World-Wide
NLD
USA
GBE
IRL
CAN
AUS
DEU
DNK
BEL
NOR
SWE
CHE
FRA
ABW
BRA
AUT
ARE
ROU
IND
The Lost World
0
10
20
30
40
50
60
Nr of contributors per country

# Hall of shame

To all who submitted and/or contributed and used '*on-premise*' instead of '*on-premises*' or '*on-prem*'. Don't worry, we've made sure everything got corrected, except for one: let's see if you can find it.

**Shame on you**

**On-premises software** (abbreviated as "on-prem" or **incorrectly** said as "on-premise") is installed and runs on computers on the premises of the person or organization using the software, rather than at a remote facility such as a server farm or Cloud. On-premises software is sometimes referred to as "shrink-wrap" software, and off-premises software is commonly called "Software-as-a-Service" ("SaaS") or "Cloud computing".

# Hall of fame

To all who submitted and/or contributed in other ways

**We salute you**

Names are listed in *alphabetical* order

Adam Osborne
Aaron Parker
Adam Yarborough
Adin Ermie
Adnan Hendricks
Alexander Tate
Andrei Vlad
Anonymous
Anton van Pelt
Arman Shara
Bart Jacobs
Bas Stapelbroek
Bas van Kaam
Benjamin Crill
Benny Tritsch
Bill Gates
Bill Sempf
Bob Molenaar
Bram Wolfs
Brian Madden
Brian Timp
Carl Stalhood
Chaitanya
Chris Hoff
Chris Howard
Chris Marks
Chris Twiest
Christiaan Brinkhoff
Cláudio Rodrigues
Danny van Dam
Daryl Plummer
Dave Brett
David Wilkinson
Dennis Smith
Dennis Span
DJ Eshelman
Edwin Houben
Eltjo van Gulik
Eric Kuiper
Eric van Klaveren
Frank Recker
Gabe Knuth
George Kuruvilla
George Spiers
Greg Shields
Gustaf Westerlund
Hans Kraaijeveld
Hans Last
Harry Bos
Henry David Thoreau
Henry Heres
Igor van der Burgh
Ivan de Mes
Jack Lee
Jack Madden
James Kindon
James Ma
James O'Regan
James Rankin
Jamil Talib
Jan Bakker
Jan de Vries
Jan Hendrik Meier
Jason Samuel
Jasper Kraak
Jeff Pitsch
Jim Moyle
Jo Harder
Johan v. Amersfoort
John Doe
Kanwal Khipple
Kees Baggerman
Kevin Howell
Kevin Goodman
Kristin Griffin
Larry Ellison
Leee Jeffries
Maarten Caus
Marc Andreessen
Marcel Kornegoor
Marcel Meurer
Marcin Policht
Marius Sandbu
Mark Plettenberg
Martijn Verheij
Martin Therkelsen
Martin Zugec
Matthijs vd Berg
Michel Roth
Michelle Gilbert
Mike Nelson
Mitch Meade
Ned Bellavance
Neil McLoughlin
Nick Casagrande
Nick Visser
Niels Kok
Patrick Coble
Patrick van den Born
Rachel Berry
Rasmus Raun-Nielsen
René Bigler
Robin Hobo
Rody Kossen
Ronnie Hamilton
Rory Monaghan
Ruben Spruijt
Rutger de Boer
Ryan Ververs-Bijkerk
Saadallah Chebaro
Saar Gillai
Sacha Thomet
Samuel Legrand
Sander Bruijs
Sander Noordijk
Sarah Lean
Scott Manchester
Scott McNealy
Scott Osborne
Shane O'Neill
Shawn Bass
Simon Binder
Socrates
Stefan Georgiev
Steve Buchanan
Steve Elgan
Steve Greenberg
Steve Jobs
Steve Noel
Thomas Poppelgaard
Tobias Kreidl
Tom Gamull
Tom Siebel
Ton de Vreede
Trentent Tye
Trond E. Haavarstein
Ufuk Koçak
William Arthur Ward
Wouter Kursten
Yoda

# About us

### *Christiaan Brinkhoff*

Christiaan Brinkhoff works as Cloud Architect and Technology Evangelist for the Windows Virtual Desktop and FSLogix team at Microsoft (ExtOps) and is the owner of christiaanbrinkhoff.com IT Consulting. In addition to his work, he shares his passion for Cloud innovation by speaking at large international conferences, writing articles for vendors and external community programs, such as VDILIKEAPRO, WhatMatrix, as well as on his website. This community-related work got him the privilege to achieve the following three – Microsoft Most Valuable Professional (MVP) for Microsoft Azure, Citrix Technology Professional (CTP), VMware vExpert vendor awards. There are currently only five people in the world that have all these titles combined.

### *Bas van Kaam*

Bas works as a Senior Business Consultant and Cloud Technologist for Salomon IT Solutions. He is the founder and owner of basvankaam.com where he shares his work and thoughts as an independent blogger/analyst on all things EUC, Cloud and tech-related. Bas is the author of over 300 blog posts, the book *Inside Citrix: The FlexCast Management Architecture*, multiple (ultimate) cheat sheets and eBooks, and has spoken at numerous national and international events across the globe. Because of his community involvement throughout the years, he has earned many different community/vendor awards. Furthermore, he's a father of three wonderful kids (Julia, Sophie and Mex), and a sports nut – running in particular.

# General views & recommendations

***Submitted by:***

**Name:** Chris Marks **Country:** Great Britain **Job role:** Sr. SE
**Company:** Nutanix

in www.linkedin.com/in/chrismarks

@ChrisJMarks

*Note that these are two submissions merged into one.*

Don't just "Follow the Crowd to the Cloud"

**Everyone is in "the Cloud", I must be the last one left!?**

Today, most organizations will be consuming Software-as-a-Service (SaaS) or Platform-as-a-Service (PaaS) in some form. For SaaS and PaaS, much of the Cloud orchestration (if there is any) is invisible to you. As a consumer, you only experience the resulting "service" and pay for what you use.

This can be incredibly convenient, but it does not mean that everyone has everything running within a Cloud-orchestrated environment; it just means that most organizations are doing something which involves the use of Cloud services. This is where statements like "98% of companies are in the Cloud" come from.

Some organizations will need to continue as they are for a while, whilst they get other things sorted out. This is ok, too – your business is your priority. Many applications do not play nicely with a true Cloud operating model today.

The model relies on workloads which are able to deal with operations on a dynamic sliding scale. Applications may have dependencies on particular services which are difficult to replicate in a Cloud model right now. This is where many organizations see value and lower transformational risk from a Hybrid Cloud approach.

Rather than say, “How fast can we get to the Cloud?”, the more important questions should be:

1. What does your changing business need from IT?
2. Will a Cloud Operating Model help deliver better value or increased competitiveness?
3. What elements of a Cloud approach would be of greatest benefit to you?
4. How will you make more money or save costs by doing this?

I’ve seen companies who really flourish with a Cloud Operating Model, but those who have been most successful have either made sure they can either orchestrate or automate workloads themselves effectively or; made sure that they can exploit those Cloud services which specifically address their needs.

Remember: Cloud is not **where** you put your IT stuff, it is **how** you operate it. There is a lot of misconception on this point alone.

In 2016, Dropbox moved most of their data and services from a public Cloud provider into their own dedicated platform. Does this mean that they moved “out of the Cloud”?

No. Their services are architected in pretty much the same way. They just worked out that, at that point in time, it was better for their business to operate their own Cloud Architecture. Have they abandoned public Cloud?

No. They still utilize it for many aspects of what they do. They’ve just worked out that, as their business has transformed, elements of their business are a great fit for the public Cloud and some elements are better served by something within their complete control. They have determined that this hybrid approach is best for their business right now.

The most important thing when looking at any technology decision is to keep your own business in mind. Saying you are "going to the Cloud" for the sake of external credibility is understandable, just be prepared for one tricky question:

"Why?"

**Why Cloud is not a Strategy**

Contentious though it may be to say, I'm going to come right out and say it. If you are creating a "Cloud strategy", the chances are you are starting in the wrong place. You may have fallen into the same trap as those who had a "VDI Strategy" or "[Insert IT Vendor here] Strategy".

***"If you've started with the technology, you've already lost focus of your business requirements and made the assumption that your business needs to fit the technology."*** – Chris Marks

Now I have absolutely nothing against public Cloud services and the benefits they may bring; on the contrary, public Cloud services present some great opportunities to achieve things previously not possible, but Cloud, in all its forms, a method of delivery, not a strategy. When you decide to utilize it and to what extent, it should be as a result of determining that this is best for your business, taking into account your specific requirements.

If you do not do this, you do not have a strategy at all, simply a way of implementing a delivery mechanism into your business, whether or not it represents a business benefit. Be in no doubt, though – considering Cloud Services and discussing them as part of your IT strategy is essential to establish the best approach for your organization.

**Business, Business, Business**

Rather than creating a siloed strategy for Cloud, a more business-focused approach would be to develop your existing strategy and see where adoption of Cloud services could provide benefits to the business. This is not a Cloud strategy – this is still your IT strategy.

There is nothing wrong at all with a hybrid approach.

A "Cloud strategy" often makes the assumption that public Cloud is all good. For many of your workloads, a local or hosted infrastructure delivery method may give you better performance, lower cost and more control. For some workloads, a Cloud service delivers greater benefits. There is nothing wrong with combining these delivery methods at all.

**"Cloud is about how you do computing, not where you do computing."**

– Paul Maritz

There is also nothing wrong with making choices today, which you alter later, as you are restricted today with applications in use or regulations which will take time to replace or update. Many organizations make decisions to place services such as Test or DR into the public Cloud, for example – this can make a lot of sense if these environments can be brought up and down as required and the services are only charged when powered on.

Powering down public Cloud services can deliver lower costs relative to the previous method of purchasing duplicate hardware for Test and DR. However, this does not necessarily assume your production infrastructure is best suited to a public Cloud approach (that, of course, is down to your business requirements).

A hybrid approach could help deliver your strategy for quite some time as a result.

## In Summary

Determine where public Cloud services fit now, and what they could do in the future. It's important to work out what is holding you back on delivering business benefits today – and deliver a strategy to resolve this. This may involve public Cloud services today; it may not. It's almost certain to involve Cloud Services in the longer term, but your specific requirements should determine this.

Cloud service adoption will continue to grow, that is not in doubt. But do what is right for you, at the right time: do not lose sight of what your business needs you to deliver and when.

***Submitted by:***

**Name:** Alexander Tate **Country:** US **Company:** CenturyLink

in www.linkedin.com/in/alex-tate-12b3387

**On the Cloud both private and public Hypervisors and more.**

Most people that you are going to work with absolutely and positively hate change. They fear it, run from it, hide from it, and will not hesitate to find the biggest cliff to give you a nice shove off when suggesting it.

Change means leaving the comfort zone and learning or doing something we are unaccustomed to. Now you, the reader, you enjoy change, embrace it, welcome it, beat it with a hammer and tell it to come back for more.

You must find the middle ground in which to initiate these conversations with older business models and older models of architecture and through methodologies.

**On proving your point, and showing that someone else is in the wrong.**

While we all know this is how we operate and do things in a civilized world, it's best not to do this in the real world. Approaching this subject is touchy, people get angry fast, throw tables, chairs, hammers, etc.

To compound this, most managers, VPs and anyone very high up will 90% of the time side with the temper tantrum going on just to diffuse the situation and coddle the one bringing the roof down. A strategy less prone to having this type of reaction is the length of rope.

Give them the rope, keep feeding them the rope while offering advice, suggestions that taking more rope is not a good idea and maybe an alternative method should be used (e.g. provide some documentation, best practices, etc.).

If they keep taking the rope, let them and then Darwin takes over at some point, metaphorically speaking. This ensures you have done everything to steer things the right way and did so in a non-disruptive method which should get you out of the hotseat when the real fireworks erupt.

Grab some popcorn and your beverage of choice and watch when that happens, it's usually a heck of a show.

**Guidelines for less headache, and angry ape tendencies when beginning a project**

1. Listen to the Stakeholders, Project Managers, Developers, etc. Listen to them and be attentive and engaging even if inside your Architect mind you fundamentally disagree and would never do anything they are saying.

2. Reference Guideline 1 above, DO NOT challenge those parties listed in a meeting everyone is at. By challenge I mean object, differ from opinion, any shape form or narrative display that you don't believe their Alpha status job production.

Nerds and their cohorts are very ego driven and when they are in packs, they turn feral. When isolated they can be reasoned with and domesticated. (Season 6 Episode 10 of *South Park* is a play on words on the above, albeit slightly different.)

3. ALWAYS and I mean ALWAYS compliment someone's submission before you even think to disagree with it or suggest alternate viewpoints (see fragile ego statement above).

You will get a far better response when people see you appreciate their value add and therefore will be more receptive to the ideas you bring.

4. K.I.S.S.: do it, live by it, die by it. Do not let anyone detract from that philosophy no matter what you are building, apps, public/private Cloud, networking, ADFS. The success or failure of your project will largely depend on that concept and how you are able to keep it applied.

5. Document everything. Go back and read that again. Once more: yup, you guessed it, read it again. DOCUMENT EVERYTHING!!

It doesn't matter how small a detail or trivial, everything in time order and design aspect, known issues, problem resolution, etc. You do not want to be fielding issues for your completed projects from Operations Management and the Service Level groups for the entirety of your career.

**"There's no way *that* company exists in a year."**

- Tom Siebel

Back in 2001 on *Salesforce.com*

***Submitted by:***

**Name:** Nick Visser **Country:** Netherlands **Job role:** Cloud Solution Architect EMEA **Company:** Insight

www.linkedin.com/in/nick-visser-54181763

www.understandthe.cloud

Cloud technology allows all of us to hop on that train of (quick) innovation and makes our daily life more simple. There is no simple answer in who has the best Cloud technologies, it is still all about the companies or people's requirements!

Create a (internal) community for adopting the Cloud and make sure your ambassadors know what it's like to "feel" the Cloud journey. Cloud is the enabler for (work) life 2.0! Cloud is a company-driven community, not only an IT-driven community.

***Submitted by:***

**Name:** Bart Jacobs **Country:** Belgium **Job role:** Consultant **Company:** BJ IT Comm.V.

www.linkedin.com/in/jacobsb

@CloudSparkle

**Asking the right questions**

The very first and very last question one should be asking is: "Why?" Asking "Why?" sometimes seems to be a lost form of art nowadays.

Never assume anything, never take anything for granted. And please, don't take any decision, small or large, because "they" said so. In all my years in consulting, I've never met "they", or better "them". What might have worked for others may result in a complete disaster in your environment.

And yes, asking "Why?" won't keep you from making mistakes. Mistakes will happen, and they can even be a good thing: when you ask yourself "Why did it go wrong?" and by answering that question, learn from your mistakes. Don't be afraid to fail, but turn those moments into learning experiences. You'll never make the same mistake twice.

***Submitted by:***

**Name:** Johan van Amersfoort **Country:** Netherlands

 www.vhojan.nl

 @vHojan

***"Running Any App on Any Device by Any User is great, but just because you can run AutoCAD on your smartphone, doesn't mean you should."***
– Johan van Amersfoort

***Submitted by:***

**Name:** Wouter Kursten **Country:** Netherlands **Job role:** Consultant **Company:** Retouw.nl

 www.nl.linkedin.com/in/wouter-kursten

 www.retouw.nl

 @Magneet_NL

The first question should always be what problem you are trying to solve. Based on the fact that the Cloud can never be a goal, but a means to reach that goal.

***Submitted by:***

**Name:** Michel Roth **Country:** Netherlands **Job role:** Director EMEA FSLogix & Windows Virtual Desktop Sales **Company:** Microsoft

 www.linkedin.com/in/michelroth

 @michelroth

Over the last few years the limits of the Profile Management approach have been reached. Specifically, there are a couple of very specific reasons why the managing of the Profile is going the way of the dodo.

1. The types of applications have changed. These days it is very common for applications to (require you to) drag along heaps of user data. Traditional files-based Profile Management tools are either incapable or horribly inefficient in persisting this user data.
2. Customers on average have (a lot) more applications than 10 years ago. No matter how you slice or dice it, you need to spend time and money figuring out how you persist with the settings associated with these application – which costs way more money and time than anybody wants to spend on "just getting an application to work"
3. Management is out. The industry has pivoted from locking down and managing the environment to providing the business with a productivity platform that is open and unmanaged wherever possible.

Enter the different Containers technologies. Although most people got introduced to this Container concept for persisting user data by FSLogix (now Microsoft), all major vendors have now subscribed to the concept of using block-based virtual disk technologies to persist user and application data in non-persistent environments. This approach works for all applications regardless of the number or size of the files while requiring no management – solving all of the aforementioned shortcomings of Profile Management.

***Submitted by:***

**Name:** Steve Elgan **Country:** US. **Job role:** IT Director **Company:** OneWorld Community Health Centers, Inc.

in www.linkedin.com/in/selgan

Whatever the technology, adopt it because it diminishes a limitation, not because it is the latest and greatest "thing" to adopt. Ask yourself, if we bring this technology into our organization, what rules are we going to change?

For example, take virtualization. If you introduced virtualization into your environment but continued to deploy VMs the same way you deployed physical servers (manually), you did not gain the full benefit of the technology.

When considering a new technology, it's important to consider the concept of technical debt, and determine how you are going to pay. Otherwise the fate of your organization rests in the hands of the few engineers who eventually will leave your organization.

***Submitted by:***

**Name:** Kanwal Khipple **Country:** Canada **Job role:** CEO **Company:** 2toLead

in www.linkedin.com/in/kanwalkhipple

 @kkhipple

Learn to fail fast. in this Cloud-first world, where change is not in your control, learn to adapt and prioritize the path to getting solutions to your users first. You will make mistakes. You will get feedback. Learn from what you hear and take another step forward.

***Submitted by:***

**Name:** Tobias Kreidl **Country:** US. **Job role:** Systems Architect
**Company:** Northern Arizona University

in www.linkedin.com/in/tobias-kreidl-7ab249a3

@tkreidl

Just about anything that you implement loses luster once it's completed and you've moved on to the next project.

However, before things pull you in too many other directions, take the time to review what you've done, perhaps taking more or updated notes on the process.

***"Above all, make sure that you have documented things well enough so that you and your customer, if there is one, can fully understand the process without having to reconstruct major parts of it. Don't forget the backup and disaster recovery aspects, which do not always get as much attention as they should!"*** – Tobias Kreidl

Things do happen and it's way better to be more prepared to deal with them than to have to scramble to figure out an emergency plan if none is already defined and in place. Practicing for a disaster and disaster recovery should always be part of that plan, no matter where your IT environment resides. Update and review the process periodically or whenever there has been a major change to the procedures or configurations.

***Submitted by:***

**Name:** Martijn Verheij **Country:** Netherlands **Job role:** Technical Specialist **Company:** Avensus

www.linkedin.com/in/martijnverheij

www.martijnverheij.nl

@martijnverheij

Why is the Cloud so important from an end-user's experience?

In May 2017 I decided to use my iPad as a replacement for my laptop. From that moment on my iPad became my main working device. The most important step for this replacement is the use of 'the Cloud'.

The term 'Cloud' can refer to different types of Cloud solutions. Of course, the iPad does not have a lot of physical free space to store documents and other data. So, data storage is an important Cloud service, with synchronization being the other one.

Think about synchronization of data between the iPhone and iPad. For example, a picture that I take with my iPhone needs to be pasted in, or attached to a Word document for a customer, using my iPad.

The last part is the VDI-based desktop. Because not everything can be done from an iPad. Take creating an Office 365 tenant, for example. For those types of tasks a 'Cloud' based desktop is the best solution to help me with this.

Considerations for Cloud and iPad usage:

- The Cloud synchronization service is very important when choosing a Cloud storage provider.

- The use of a Citrix (private or public Cloud) environment is also possible on an iPad. Citrix offers the X1 Mouse to make navigating easier. It's controlled by the Citrix Receiver software.
- When choosing a Cloud (storage) provider, make sure to choose one that offers data protection services like previous versions and MFA.
- Most Cloud providers offer free trial periods. Make use of these before getting a paid subscription.

***Submitted by:***

**Name:** Jeff Pitsch **Country:** US **Job role:** Sr. Solutions Architect
**Company:** Liquidware

www.linkedin.com/in/jeffpitsch

@JeffPitsch

Cloud vendors use very different names for components we are used to. For instance, networking components in the Cloud vary from vendor to vendor, and from their on-premises components.

It can be difficult to figure them out and put them all together but once you realize that the Cloud components are simply different names for what we are used to on-premises, it all starts to fall together.

**"I don't need a hard disk in my computer if I can get to the server faster… carrying around these non-connected computers is Byzantine by comparison."** – Steve Jobs.

**Sponsored content**

**Now, Windows Virtual Desktop.**
When Microsoft announced its Windows Virtual Desktop, they included us as a "leading partner" for the solution. Our development and product teams have been working with Microsoft for more than 18 months in the development of this solution. We have never felt so honored to be part of a product development team, and we have been part of many across our history.

**Cloud Workspace**
Managed Platform is a turnkey service that runs your Cloud Workspace environment... from app installation and Office 365 integration to anti-virus, backup, Active Directory and more. We support deployments in Azure, GCP, AWS and Private Cloud. Use our simple, lightning-fast migration solutions to convert your end-users into the Cloud quickly and easily.

***You Stay in Control.*** Use our single-pane-of-glass portal, my. *CloudJumper*, for deploying and managing your end-users. It keeps you in control of all users, security settings, groups and servers. You also use it to track tickets, review invoices, and check performance metrics.

**Request a demo here**
https://cloudjumper.com/cloudworkspace

Or contact us at hello@cloudjumper.com or call 844.645.6789 for a free, fully supported trial.

***Submitted by:***

**Name:** Kees Baggerman **Country:** Netherlands **Job role:** Technical Director **Company:** Nutanix

www.linkedin.com/in/keesbaggerman

www.blog.myvirtualvision.com

@KBaggerman

Enabling Cloud services is easy, moving off Cloud services is much harder. Think about this and make sure you know which implications you'll have when you're moving away from a particular Cloud service (either moving to another Cloud service or on-premises).

***"Before you start with your Cloud strategy, you should already have an exit strategy."*** – Kees Baggerman

***Submitted by:***

**Name:** George Spiers **Country:** Ireland **Job role:** EUC Architect **Company:** Novosco

www.linkedin.com/in/jgs10

www.jgspiers.com

@JGSpiers

To be successful with a Cloud deployment, it is key that you understand exactly what your customer wants and expects from a move to the Cloud. Once you have this understanding, you cross-reference the desirables against what the Cloud solution offers. This avoids any hiccups later in the deployment and allows you to choose the best Cloud solution upfront.

***Submitted by:***

**Name:** Niels Kok **Country:** Netherlands **Company:** Avensus **Job role:** Technical Specialist

www.linkedin.com/in/niels-kok-79823360

www.avansus.nl

**SCCM vs. Microsoft Intune**

I would like to talk about traditional enrollment method (SCCM) vs. a modern enrollment method (Intune) or a combination of those (Hybrid, SCCM & Intune). I would like to explain cases in which I think you should use SCCM, and which cases you should use Intune. This choice depends on a few variables, some of which are:

1. Numbers of offices and the size of those offices (users per office)
2. Applications (SaaS, published Apps, Client-Server)
3. Document management (Fileserver, SharePoint, Business Application)

For example:

*Traditional IT infrastructure*: Everybody works at the office. Their core business applications use the client-server model which requires that the client of this application needs a low latency connection to the database. Document management is being handled by a file server and the User Profiles are stored there as well. I would advise this organization to use SCCM for endpoint deployment.

*Modern IT infrastructure*: Users often work from home or at client's offices. Most of the applications are web-based or published apps. Document management is handled by SharePoint or another web-based document management system, and personal documents are in OneDrive. In this situation I would advise Microsoft Intune.

There is also the possibility to use a hybrid solution. In this case the endpoint is available in Active Directory and Azure Active Directory. This feature is currently in preview in Microsoft Intune.

I would advise this for organizations which are transitioning to the Cloud or have some users which often work from home or on business trips. The choice of software for endpoint enrollment very much depends on how your IT infrastructure is built or how you want to restructure this.

***Submitted by***:

**Name:** Adam Yarborough **Country:** US. **Job role:** Systems Administrator

 @LittleToyRobots

The planning stages of a Cloud migration is a great time to plan for the network segregation of legacy applications. Some workloads will never translate to Cloud efficiently, for whatever reason, but you can use the transition to a new network topology as a catalyst to sandbox those legacy systems.

***"We all have had production machines that just can't die for some reason, so why not use a cut-over or maintenance window to change the way they're accessed as well?"*** – Adam Yarborough

***Submitted by:***

**Name:** Marcel Meurer **Country:** Germany **Job role:** Microsoft Azure MVP **Company:** Sepago

in www.linkedin.com/in/marcel-meurer-15b46b98

 @MarcelMeurer

IoT – or why it is important to save as much data as possible

“Data are the new gold of small, medium and large businesses.” With this statement Florian Stadtfeld and I have started several workshops around data, analytics and AI in our customer environment and in the partner landscape during the last few months.

What almost sounds like a phrase sometimes seems to be “difficult” in the context of data protection and other regulations – primarily in the EU. We are often asked: “Is that ok?” and often the answer is: “It depends.”

It’s easier with IoT data – at least if technical data are in focus without any dependency on people. Regardless of this, one question is always asked in IoT workshops.

*Which data should be stored in which intervals? I don’t want to store insignificant data – that generates unnecessary costs.*

I myself have a very clear answer to this question that I would like to share. But first the context is important in order to be able to classify the question and my answer. I support enterprise companies and smaller manufacturers running their IoT projects: from the very first workshop to the completion of the project. The devices/sensors are of different kinds:

- Building control systems with many existing sensors
- Man-sized bandsaws for sawing stones and marble
- Stone mills to grind rocks
- Cutting time measurement for industrial blades
- Special sensors for flow rates, rotation, power measurement ...
- "Cloud-born" sensors that can use Wi-Fi connection natively
- ...

The motivation for using IoT is usually clear: new business models and better services. Many other motivations could be mentioned but are often included in these two aspects. Here is an example:

**New business models**

- Sale of a machine's capacity as a service: X $ per 60.000 meters cutting of sheet metal (incl. wear material)
- Turbine flying hours (instead of purchase)
- Combined heat and power unit for rent: price per kWh output incl. wear material and maintenance
- ...

**Service**

- Predictive Maintenance: The prediction of possible failures of a machine part and its timely repair
- Energy optimization for building – for example, by automatic control of climate systems based on the forecast weather
- Simplification of maintenance by a complete documentation of operating conditions (recognition of failure causes instead of only repairing things)
- ...

IoT always includes an effective storage of large amounts of data and data analytics – especially if the interpretation of this data is necessary to get further results.

- An example: A long-term measurement of the case frequency of a large bandsaw shows a correlation to a possible imminent brake of the band. The frequency increases over time.
- The action: The band is replaced directly after the current cutting process.
- The advantage: The band does not tear the material, which is not destroyed, and the band does not have to be removed costlily.

Other data derivations are not as trivial as in the example above. Hundreds of factors/measured values over a long period of time can provide information about the behavior of machines/systems. These relationships can be so complex that it's too difficult to be understood by a human.

In such cases AI systems are used which can be trained accordingly to predict the state of a system autonomously (e.g. they can warn that a system will fail within the next 20-48 hours by a probability of 86%).

Today AI and machine learning are no longer strong hypes and topics – they are standard (even if a trained neural network still has something of a black box). Machine learning has in its name "the challenge" in terms of data in IoT projects:

A machine learning model needs to be trained and requires a large amount of classified data. 'Large' in this case means data collected over a longer period (if you have even more data the model can work with a higher precision). 'Large' also means many different sensors that play a role in the model: Directly and indirectly. And this is not always obvious.

This derivation also leads directly to the correct answer to the question above:

***"It is important to store as much data as possible in appropriate short intervals. Even if there is no business case currently, no marketing approach, or if a certain sensor seems to be unimportant."***
– Marcel Meurer

My reason for claiming this: If we develop a business model based on AI in 6 months, then we might need exactly these data. If we don't collect them today, they will be lost for the future.

The use of Cloud technologies supports this approach: I use managed platform services from the Microsoft Azure Cloud for IoT, AI, data storage and processing. Especially storage of data in Cloud structures is very efficient and cost-effective.

***Submitted by:***

**Name:** Steve Greenberg **Country:** US. **Job role:** President/Principal Architect **Company:** Thin Client Computing

www.linkedin.com/in/greenbergsteve

www.thinclient.net

@stevegreenberg

**Know What You are Doing Before you Act in the Cloud!**

Cloud is often said to be nebulous or vague, but it is not. There is a very useful definition provided by NIST in the US:

https://nvlpubs.nist.gov/nistpubs/Legacy/SP/nistspecialpublication800-145.pdf

The most efficient model is Software as a Service followed by Platform as a Service. When you consume a particular function you need directly, the scale of Cloud brings great benefits. The least efficient, and most expensive, model is Infrastructure-as-a-Service since you are paying to use someone else's compute, storage and network resources to run your workloads.

It is too common to assume the "Cloud" means someone else will simply take the burden of my systems away from me. Every day I hear statements such as, "Let's move it to the Cloud so we don't have to worry about it anymore," and nothing could be further from the truth.

The actual definition contains nothing about the location of resources, service providers, subscription licensing or deployment frameworks. Cloud computing is a delivery model with particular characteristics as follows:

- On-Demand Self-Service
- Broad Network Access
- Resource Pooling
- Rapid Elasticity
- Measured Service

What it distinctly does NOT promise or specify is:

- Security Assurances
- Lower Cost
- Easy Deployment
- Excellent match for your workloads
- Whether or not it takes place on or off premises

Cloud computing is an approach with a set of powerful tools that help when leveraged thoughtfully, and create havoc when applied improperly. Learn these tools well, examine each of your needs, and apply the right tool for the right job!

***Submitted by:***

**Name:** Benjamin Crill **Country:** US. **Job role:** Principal Consultant Architect **Company:** Hogan Consulting Group

www.linkedin.com/in/benjamincrill

www.icrill.com

@benjamincrill

Always remember that Cloud is an operational model, not a hosting infrastructure. You can have Cloud on-prem. It is about self-service, automation, and flexibility. If you just put app servers and desktops on Azure/AWS and still provision them manually, your environment isn't Cloud. Cloud should change your processes and make things more consistent, repeatable, and expandable for users.

***Submitted by:***

**Name:** James Ma **Country:** US. **Job role:** Citrix Architect **Company:** Cloudma

www.linkedin.com/in/jameswma

@jameswma

If you want the organization to adopt a new technology / service / method, teach everyone about it, especial key players. The masses only commit to what they know and what feels safe.

**"The mediocre teacher tells. The good teacher explains. The superior teacher demonstrates. The great teacher inspires."** - William Arthur Ward

***Submitted by**:*

**Name:** Henry Heres **Country:** Netherlands **Company:** Technical Fellows

in www.linkedin.com/in/henryheres

www.technicalfellows.nl

@hereshenry

**Scribble dibble doo**

*Scribble #1*

When in doubt, trace your flow! Always know where you start and where you will end in a network, e.g. follow the packet. And remember, when you assume you make an ass out of u and me.

*Scribble #2*

Don't be afraid or too high and mighty before contacting support of vendors, basically if you don't log it, they won't know it. Even the smallest "issue" or "bug" is worth the effort.

**"The computer industry is the only industry that is more fashion-driven than women's fashion. Maybe I'm an idiot, but I have no idea what anyone is talking about. What is it? It's complete gibberish. It's insane. When is this idiocy going to stop? We'll make Cloud computing announcements. I'm not going to fight this thing. But I don't understand what we would do differently in the light of Cloud."** – Larry Ellison

***Submitted by:***

**Name:** Robin Hobo **Country:** Netherlands **Job role:** Solution Architect Mobility **Company:** Comparex

www.linkedin.com/in/robinhobo

www.robinhobo.com

@robinhobo

As a Solution Architect Mobility, I have a lot of meetings with customers who are exploring whether Cloud is the next step for them. Given my function, this usually concerns the possibility to manage different types of devices from the Cloud, but with some regularity I also get the question: "We want to get rid of our hosted environment (RDS / VDI), can you help us with this?

***"In most cases, research tells us that this is not yet possible for the customer in question. This has mainly to do with necessary 'legacy' applications that are not available as an SaaS service or can be moved to the Cloud."*** – Robin Hobo

However, for the first point it is possible in most cases. There are several products on the market that make it possible to manage mobile devices such as phones and tablets from the Cloud. And not just phones and tablets, but also Windows 10 and macOS devices.

This allows the customer to manage these devices in a modern way, from the Cloud, without the need for the device to be connected to a local network.

For this book, I would like to give you some advice on which points should be taken into account during the product selection, but also during its design.

## Native Apps or Managed App Container

After explaining the possibilities within an Enterprise Mobility Management (EMM) solutions, I always ask the customer: "What are the requirements for accessing company data from a mobile device?" Based on the answer, the choice can be made whether MDM functionality is sufficient (and thus making use of the native applications), or whether a Managed App Container is needed.

Although a Managed App Container is more secure, adoption by the end-user is very important and can cause problems. (I've seen projects fail on this part.)

Test with multiple Mobility Management solutions (if possible) and involve the end-user during a pilot phase.

When a Managed App Container is needed make sure that the required apps that need to be managed are available for the Enterprise Mobility Management solution in question, or that you have access to the unsigned source of the app (IPA for iOS, APK for Android) so that you can sign it yourself for integration.
The choice for native apps or the managed app container is fundamental to the rest of the configuration.

## Conditional Access

Always configure Conditional Access to corporate data such as files and email. Most common Conditional Access rules are that the device needs to be managed and compliant or that data can only be accessed via a managed application.

Without Conditional Access it doesn't make any sense to apply security settings on a managed device, while an end-user can configure his mail on an unmanaged device without any restrictions.

### Cloud vs. On-premises

Most EMM solutions are available as Cloud service and on-premises installation. If there are no company policies that require the on-premises installation, I always recommend the Cloud service. In many cases the Cloud solution has more features than the on-premises version and the Cloud service is updated faster (in some cases weekly).

The on-premises updates will become available (not always with every new feature), but after a few weeks or even months. Updating on-premises installations can create a large management burden for the IT department: with the Cloud service the update maintenance is carried out by the EMM vendor.

**"Mobile phones are misnamed. They should be called gateways to human knowledge."**

– Ray Kurzweil

***Submitted by:***

**Name:** Rasmus Raun-Nielsen **Country:** Denmark **Job role:** Sr. System Consultant **Company:** Conecto A/S

www.linkedin.com/in/rasmus-raun-nielsen-6592726

@RBRConecto

My top 6

**Have a clear goal**

Every project should start by defining a specific, well-described, reasonable and achievable goal. This goal needs to be verified both during the implementation and after – for instance, economy, which is one of the (big) parameters and obviously needs to be addressed before starting a project, but also during as well as after the project is finished.

***"The nature of the Cloud makes VM-instances and -pricing fluctuating. New VM-instances are introduced regularly and are influencing pricing, so what is not feasible today may be a real possibility tomorrow."*** – Rasmus Raun-Nielsen

**Focus**

It may sound obvious, but when talking End-User Computing, remember to have the end-user in focus. When you start designing (especially for the Cloud), it's easy to get confused and sidetracked because of the number of possibilities and options. I use "divide and conquer" as a way for me to remember to filter out all that is irrelevant and make it easier to get an overview and digest the remaining information (which, by the way, also can be effective in other aspects of life – for instance, when looking for a new car or building a house).

This, together with a specified and well-described goal, will make it easier to stay on the right path to success. It may sound like a cliché or a broken record, but it is essentially as easy as this: Stay focused on the target/goal

**Prepare to lose (a little) control – and accept it…**

The Cloud is "just another datacenter", which means you don't get to worry about cooling, security parameters, hardware compatibility, upgrade cycles, service windows, etc. This, however, comes at the cost of control.

**Planning – "Always have an exit strategy"**

Do not expect your environment to exist in a static, stable state forever. Changes will come: Some will be controllable and others will not, so as in all aspects of life always have (at least) a plan B... By keeping things in an open and well-defined format, it's easier to migrate or change parts of the environment to new solutions that may be a better fit.

***"Every time I move from one Cloud to another, if I have to refractor [rewrite] my applications: that is not very efficient or cost-effective and doesn't give [the agency] agility, he added. Agency managers might not be thinking a lot about exit strategies now. But they should be incorporating them in their concept of operation plans."***

– Bill Rowan @MeriTalk

**Latency – "No one enjoys being forced to wait."**

Aim to minimize any (potential) latency: Some aspects of latency can and must be minimized by correct decisions in the design: others are not possible to affect unless you have full control of specific layers in the stack. In this case you need the issues to be identified and mitigated on a different layer or layers of the stack on which you have control.

**Verification – "Do not assume anything: Verify!"**

Specifically for situations where you have limited control, Murphy's Law dictates that changes will happen and you may not always get informed in a timely fashion, so make sure to have those web URLs with operational status in your Favorites bar.

When in production, remember to keep an eye on the cost! Whatever is not being utilized is practically money thrown out of the window (no pun intended). Investigate any possibility of shutting down VM-instances which are not being utilized.

When in doubt, ask! Nobody is able to know everything, but chances are that someone may have come across your specific question or issue. Use the support or hotline, search for information in the communities, but don't expect people to do the searching and information gathering for you unless you pay them for it.

***Submitted by:***

**Name:** Simon Binder **Country:** Sweden **Job role:** Principal Solutions Architect **Company:** Atea

www.linkedin.com/simonbinderatea

www.kneedeepintech.com

@Bindertech

When it comes to Cloud, and IT in general, we often try to find the best breed for every single service. This unfortunately often ends up in a mishmash of technologies, vendors, techniques and languages. To simplify this, begin by gathering your entire IT department and have an open discussion on: "Who should be our primary vendor of IT?"

This could be any vendor, Cloud, networking, devices, CRM – it doesn't matter. Select one, which then everyone else should try to build a good service on top of.

***"Every other vendor after your strategic one should be able to implement with the first. That's how you build the best possible ecosystem for your IT, that's how you build a successful Cloud journey, that's how you build a great experience for you as an admin."*** – Simon Binder

In terms of Cloud, do the same. Choose one Cloud to start with, and then integrate the rest as well as possible.

I do believe that you in the long run will be way better off by doing that, rather than taking the best of breed service and trying to integrate those. It's the best integrations that win. Because if the Cloud works together, everybody wins.

***Submitted by:***

**Name:** Matthijs van den Berg **Country:** Netherlands **Job role:** Manager Systems Engineering Nutanix **Company:** Nutanix

 www.linkedin.com/in/matthijsvandenberg

@matthijs_berg

Almost 2000 years ago Marcus Aurelius wrote: “The impediment to action advances action. What stands in the way becomes the way.” Is this applicable to modern IT and the changes we’re facing?

The first part of the quote, “The impediment to action advances action”, is all about change. When we are unable to achieve our goals, we seek new ways.

I consider this a result of striving being the nature of humankind. We see this happening in organizations every day. When our internal IT department can’t deliver what we want (in time), the organization will find other ways to achieve its goals.

The term “Shadow IT” has grown from this desire to achieve goals. Most organizations want an IT solution that is agile, so it can adapt to changing business needs.

Security and cost are important factors for business continuity and successful business cases, but in my experience there are few to no companies that ask for Virtual machines, Containers, LUNs or a certain server brand. I consider them to be “what’s in the way” when trying to achieve the business goals. We might need them, but they should be derived from the end goal.

The second part of the quote, “What stands in the way becomes the way”, is about how to change. Many organizations initiate projects to start new lines of business or improve existing ones.

There are many milestones on this road to a new product, IT being one of them. If we solely focus on the IT part of this road, we see a lot of IT departments that have lost focus on the business aspirations of their company.

Technology has become their main driver to change. They ran into an issue in the past – for example, not being able to provision new servers fast enough – and have adopted virtualization to counter that. That was a great change for many organizations, but it became THE way over time. “New and cool” features are dictating IT roadmaps.

This leads to IT departments that are not in search of a new platform to support the business, but are blinded by products and brand names that they have built their careers on. What once stood in the way has become the way.

I personally see a lot of organizations struggling with this. Management wants an agile solution, where the IT department is still refreshing existing solutions and adding layers like containers, software-defined networking, and automation. A lot of outsourcing and Cloud adoption comes from this discrepancy between management and IT goals.

Before you start your next project ask yourself: Do we really need this and where does this benefit my company? Consider ROI as what defines the business case. If we don’t constantly ask ourselves how we contribute to positive business outcomes, IT might just become another bump in the road of the company’s way to success.

***Submitted by:***

**Name:** Brian Timp **Country:** Netherlands **Job role:** Senior Technical Consultant EUC **Company:** Proact Netherlands

 www.linkedin.com/in/briantimp

 @briantimp

When moving to Cloud services, the Cloud can be considered from three different angles: employee perspective, technology perspective, and business perspective.

Today's businesses are undergoing a rapid transformation. Companies and businesses must digitalize to offer improved user experience and achieve operational benefits that are only available to businesses able to harness the disruptive opportunities that new technologies can provide. More than any other innovation, Cloud services have become a major catalyst for digitalization.

Moving to Cloud services requires a different way of thinking. While there are many benefits and opportunities that come with using Cloud services, it requires substantial adjustments to behavior. Many people are naturally reluctant for new things, but it's important to help them understand where they need to go and why. Once people see the big picture: the Cloud is no longer an obstacle, but a window of opportunity.

So the question is: What this journey to the Cloud looks like? Moving to the Cloud is a big change for any business. Lift and shift workloads to the Cloud and assume everything will work fine?

That is not going to work; even if it does, it will not guarantee the business value and outcome from such a move. With a clear vision and an overall strategy, you can reduce or even eliminate barriers to the Cloud world.

Moving to Cloud services will affect every business unit and it's important to understand the impact of it. So first explore the benefits, seeking customer needs and enhancing employee skills. Roles and responsibilities may need to be redefined, and working on communities containing people with different skill sets makes more sense than having teams working on isolated products with no integration, communication or shared goal.

The first perspective in this journey to the Cloud is the employee perspective. Preparing employees is important. The Cloud facilitates the unrestricted flow of work and ideas. When people realize that networks, storage, and even computers are dissolved by the Cloud, the potential for collaboration is only limited by the willingness and imagination of the employees.

Also make sure that your employees have the right skills. Since classic troubleshooting methods are not working anymore for Cloud workloads, it is vital to have the right Cloud specialists, architects and project managers to get your systems off the ground.
The second perspective is technology. Most organizations choose the hybrid Cloud model, where some resources and services are still on-premises, while others are moved to the Cloud. This choice is common when the business has many workloads on-premises, but also can benefit from using Cloud services.

With the above approach, the same service can be offered from the Cloud and on-premises at the same time. This flexibility will give you the time to migrate and move data at your own timeline. This also means a more complex infrastructure to support both.

Through this hybrid model, your business can access specific Cloud solutions that meet their needs. In your day-to-day operations, you can use Office 365 and Cloud identity, while on-premises workloads are available when security or regulation is required.

The last perspective is business. From a business perspective, the Cloud is as important as the services you are using for your core business applications.

These services, for example, get extended with Cloud identity that enables business users to access any on-premises or Cloud application using the same set of credentials, to make it more convenient for end-users, and to ensure security and compliance. Software as a Service (SaaS) is everywhere.

***"Businesses are consuming SaaS applications more than before, and having a solid Cloud-federated identity model has never been as important."***
– Brian Timp

When moving to the Cloud, the role of IT is changing. The moment will come that all (or most of) your business applications will be powered by the Cloud and the role of IT will shift from maintaining and deploying on-premises solutions, to be more business-focused. Understand what the Cloud can provide (business value) and how integration and security work. This changing role will also enable IT to hunt business opportunities and implement them by the power of the Cloud.

***Submitted by:***

**Name:** Steve Buchanan **Country:** US. **Job role:** Cloud Architect

 www.buchatech.com

 @Buchatech

These areas are key to being successful in the Cloud! #1 Modern Security Strategy, #2 Modern Network Design, #3 Cloud Governance Strategy, #4 Cloud Management Strategy, and #5 Modern Automation Strategy (IaC, Containers, Serverless).
– Microsoft MVP Steve Buchanan

***Submitted by:***

**Name:** James Rankin **Country:** Great Britain **Job role:** Technical News Hound & Consultant **Company:** james-rankin.com

www.linkedin.com/in/james-rankin-6094607

www.james-rankin.com

@james____rankin

*Note that these are three submissions merged into one.*

## A question of Cloud

Cloud computing. Cloud is everywhere, it seems. What is Cloud? According to NIST...

"Cloud computing is a model for enabling convenient, on-demand network access to a shared pool of configurable computing resources (e.g. networks, servers, storage, applications, and services) that can be rapidly provisioned and released with minimal management effort or service provider interaction."

Wow. That's a mouthful. But everywhere we look, Cloud is the big buzzword. Digital transformation insists that we embrace Cloud computing as the next evolution of our enterprise.

Microsoft, Amazon, Citrix, and VMware, among many others, are all focused on Cloud and mobility as the next logical step forward. Upstart companies like Netflix are the trailblazers, embracing the Cloud completely and putting less agile competitors like Blockbuster to the sword.

We are being fed a diet of marketing that tells us we should ignore the Cloud at our peril. Marketeers tell us things like this quote from IDC:

*"Become heavily Cloud-centric, in technology adoption and in skills, over the next several years – or find yourself stranded on the outskirts of digital transformation in your own industry."*

In response, what are the pertinent questions we should be asking to ensure that we make the right decisions for the future shape of our enterprise IT? There are many considerations that need to be taken into account, if you're to avoid becoming a Cloud casualty.

Firstly, is the future irrevocably tied to Cloud – the public Cloud – as many in marketing would have us believe? Is it good for us, or is it good for the companies providing it? Now that VMs are easy, bandwidth is faster, and hardware is cheaper, do we simply abandon everything we have in-house and move all that expertise to "the Cloud"? Is it feasible to send all of our workloads to an online hosting model?

Unfortunately, workloads are tricky things to pin down. For every Netflix, which by its very nature is ideally suited to Cloud computing, there are many other industry verticals that aren't so well suited. Real-time scientific data, super-high-res printing, trading floors, manufacturing – these are just a few examples of areas where the drawbacks of Cloud solutions may make them unsuitable for particular workloads.

Of course, everyone has some workloads that are suited to Cloud computing, email and instant messaging being two of the most fitting. If Azure has an outage and email is offline for a day, then it isn't the end of the world. Cloud services are ideal for workloads that don't need to be live 100% of the time. Even for things like back-ups, if it works 99% of the time, there won't be a huge problem.

However, if a company has a business-critical manufacturing process and loses that capability for an hour or two, there are serious ramifications for profitability.

Anything you need constant access to or that is intensely sensitive to latency is an area in which an outage will have real, damaging effects. For these workloads, it still makes more sense to run them locally.

If you're in an industry in which some workloads absolutely need to be run locally, then you have an investment in shop floor IT to make, anyway. If you already have local IT and on-premises skills, then for every workload that could be Cloud-hosted, you need to ask whether it is more feasible to run it locally or in the Cloud.

There are other questions that need to be asked as well.
It's not a technical consideration, but trust has to be central to Cloud adoption. How much do you trust Microsoft, Citrix, Google, VMware, Dropbox, Salesforce, Amazon, etc. with your data and your infrastructure? Do you trust them to act ethically when they are faced with demands from US law enforcement for access to data held in overseas jurisdictions, as both Microsoft and Google have been recently? How much do you trust agencies like GCHQ and the NSA to avoid making Cloud repositories high-value targets for espionage?

How much will it cost? There's not just the cost of bandwidth, but also the cost of running the infrastructure itself (and all the little extra costs that keep being added to it, of which Cloud providers seem to be so fond). How will that measure up to the cost of running locally? Is it possible to predict the investment you're going to have to make with any accuracy? On top of this, what do you do with the existing investment you've made in on-premises kit? Do you simply abandon it?

What will the support be like? Will you be tied to the same SLAs you get with local infrastructure? Usually on-premises support can diagnose problems quite quickly, mainly due to familiarity with the systems in use. If there's a problem with an application, they can usually address it at the source.

With a Cloud-hosted system, in which support teams invariably must manage multiple tenancies with disparate solutions in place, how long does it take to diagnose an issue? It could be the client endpoint, their router, their ISP, their account, the authentication service, the hosted application service, or the remote datacenter. Will the added complexity of the Cloud-hosted solution translate into longer delays while service is restored?

Is security necessarily better from a Cloud provider? While the chance to offload the day-to-day operational workload to someone else is a big draw of Cloud computing, it may be what gives enterprises the most cause for concern. Someone else is now handling your data, so will your data be secure?

You'd expect a Cloud provider's huge team of security experts to have more knowledge, training, and visibility than your one- or two-person IT security staff, but are they intimately familiar with every aspect of your business and every nuance of your applications? Most security approaches depend on the assumption that you're actually in control of the data you're protecting: does a Cloud-hosted solution fly in the face of this?

What does the EU's GDPR legislation hold for you if you're adopting the Cloud? Is data sovereignty an issue?

Are your data and your infrastructure going to be held hostage? Once you're "in" with a Cloud provider, can you then get out again? Should you split your infrastructure across multiple Cloud providers to ensure you can't be locked in or have the screws turned on you with price increases? If you do split the infrastructure, or if you're using something like Citrix's Azure services, where two companies provide separate layers of the infrastructure, whose throat do you strangle when something goes wrong? If you want to migrate across Cloud providers or even perform a full "Cloud regression", how do you start to manage this?

And this raises a final point. On-premises IT fails at least as much as, and possibly more than, Cloud IT does. So why do users and management generally accept occasional failures with on-premises IT, but lose their collective heads when there is a small outage on AWS or Azure?

It's not just a case of "hoping the big kids fail", although there is possibly an element of that at work. If there's a planned outage for an on-premises solution, that's just in-house IT doing what in-house IT does. But if a major Cloud host goes down, even for a short period of time, it's big news, and it invariably generates a lot of coverage. Cloud providers sell themselves on their reliability, and when that fails, it gets publicized.

There's also an element of the personal touch to in-house IT that is sadly lacking, currently, in a Cloud-based solution. A good IT department keeps everyone – users, management, third parties – in the loop. Even in those large enterprises for which regular updates need to be given, a dedicated IT department can give a sincere and business-focused response.

However, Cloud providers tend to offer canned responses that have been sanitized with the appropriate legal precautions. Their customers feel like they're being kept in the dark and jump onto social media platforms to vent their frustration, and before long the outage is on the front page of every tech website.

Cloud is great for back-ups and disaster recovery. Building disaster recovery sites is so much easier. It's great for scalability in environments that need to increase capacity rapidly at particular times (assuming you don't pay too much for it). It's also great for moving lower-impact services like email, instant messaging, and monitoring into an environment where you don't have to worry about operational overhead and hassles.

And it certainly has a big part to play in the transformation of modern IT environments that we see on the horizon. Windows 10 brings a new wave of rapid change, and it represents possibly the first iteration of the Cloudy OS of the future.

There's no "one size fits all" here; each business has unique priorities. In most cases, I believe we will see what is termed the hybrid Cloud – the amalgamation of both public and private resources – as we look to take advantage of both on-premises and Cloud-based solutions. Why? Because public and private each addresses different important issues. Essentially, every business that has a remote datacenter already has a private Cloud, and services like Azure and AWS will add a public one.

Usage of services like Azure and AWS often starts as a sandbox or test environment: a low-cost, hardware-independent way to spin up easily accessible development systems. But sometimes these test beds grow into bigger things, due primarily to the broad and rapid scalability of these hosted platforms. At this point, and after considering the points made earlier, businesses will have to decide whether or not to proceed with Cloud-based production infrastructure.

Hybrid is likely to be the way forward for the foreseeable future, although certain industries may find it easier to go all-in on Cloud than others. Your deployment decisions should be evaluated carefully in light of your unique priorities; there is no one-size-fits-all answer. Ultimately, most businesses will want to take advantage of both on-premises and Cloud-based solutions because they address different important issues. Has any technology since the mainframe truly totally replaced its predecessors? Some may well have supplemented existing tech, but none has yet fully superseded it. Cloud looks to be no different.

***Submitted by:***

**Name:** Mike Nelson **Country:** US. **Job role:** Architect

www.linkedin.com/in/nelmedia

www.geektweakers.com

@nelmedia

Want to supercharge your Azure experience and features? Here are two tips to feed your hunger for Azure coolness!

To see the latest Azure Portal UI preview, just add the word "preview" to the Azure login URL – https://preview.portal.azure.com

How about what's available for private and public previews across all of Azure? Here's how to get a listing and request access via PowerShell! (*Note – some requests may not work due to subscription whitelisting requirement by the Product Groups):

1) Open a Cloud Shell or connect to Azure in PowerShell.
2) Enter "get-azproviderfeature -ListAvailable". It will produce a long listing of features you are registered for and others you can request access to.
3) If you see one that you want to request access to, use the cmdlet "Register-AzureRmProviderFeature -FeatureName "< >" – ProviderNamespace < >
That feature will now go into a "pending" state.

If you are accepted, which may take some time, you will see a registration state of "Registered".

Check back once in a while for new features as they are added!

***Submitted by:***

**Name:** Ufuk Koçak **Country:** Netherlands **Job role:** Sr. System Engineer **Company:** Horizon IT Consulting

www.linkedin.com/in/ufukkocak

www.horizonconsulting.it

@ik_ufukkocak

My thoughts about the Cloud are as follows. Cloud is now there; it has been playing for some time and is increasingly becoming the only topic of conversation. With the current developments, it will continue to grow, and vendors will focus more on the Cloud.

It started with the Private Cloud, then you saw more of the public Cloud coming up and I expect that in about 10 years (just looking at the crystal ball) most large companies, including the government, will consist of a Hybrid Cloud environment. Hereby I expect that the majority of the IT infrastructure will run in the Cloud and that the legal challenge will be solved. I do not believe that we will escape this sooner or later.

I also compare it a bit with different stores which at some point had to do something with the internet. Those who have not acted on it in time have gone bankrupt or had to exchange the physical stores for a web store.

That's why my advice would be for organizations to get ahead of it now. Look at it, play with it, set up a survey for your employees asking how they see it, investigate the regulations, you name it. The biggest challenge I see is retraining of employees, the adaptation of employees' working methods and the landing of the employees' mindset.

Cloud is going to play a very big role in the future, so be prepared!

***Submitted by:***

**Name:** Marcel Meurer **Country:** Germany **Job role:** Business, Cloud and Data first Enthusiast – MVP Microsoft Azure **Company:** Sepago

 www.linkedin.com/in/marcel-meurer-15b46b98

 www.sepago.de/blog/author/marcel-meurer

 @MarcelMeurer

Microsoft Azure offers a lot of services, from IaaS to hundreds of different services. Managing VMs and software has been the primary tasks of IT pros. But times are changing. Today it's more important to deliver smart solutions very fast to the business which often does not work in the traditional way.

Platform services are the key. They give us the blocks to build solutions – without maintaining VMs. One of my favorite services is Azure Monitor. Azure Monitor is a personal big data container from Microsoft.

You can use it for your own data. Upload a huge amount of data, evaluate and display it in seconds. An example: I have written my own agent for Azure Monitor, which collects user satisfaction metrics on terminal servers (Windows Virtual Desktop, Citrix Worker …) and uploads them. Different metrics are connected and displayed as charts and values in the Azure Portal. And important: The solution doesn't need an SQL Server (-) or additional infrastructure – PaaS only.

But Azure Monitor is not limited to IT-based metrics and data. In another project I use Azure Monitor as a "database" for social media data. More precisely, I push Twitter tweets to it. Up to multiple thousands per hour. Within Azure Monitor I can create reports on topics and trends related to the geo-coordinates very quickly.

What do you need to start using Azure Monitor for your own data and solutions?

Deploy Azure Monitor within your Azure Subscription (hint: it's called "Log Analytics"). Upload your data via the REST API (https://docs.microsoft.com/en-us/rest/api/loganalytics/).

Start evaluating your data with the Kusto language (https://docs.microsoft.com/en-us/azure/azure-monitor/log-query/query-language).

Have fun and enjoy your big data as a service.

**"There were 5 exabytes of information created between the dawn of civilization through 2003, but that much information is now created every day."**

– Eric Schmidt

***Submitted by:***

**Name:** Gabe Knuth **Country:** US.

www.linkedin.com/in/gabeknuth

 @GabeKnuth

Over the years I've seen many companies make decisions without considering the entirety of their environment. Sometimes they were reacting (or overreacting) to situations that came up, but more often than not these companies "didn't know what they didn't know."

That's not a typo – it's absolution. How can you be expected to know the answer to a question you didn't even know you were supposed to ask? How can you know how to solve a problem that you didn't know existed? (There are limits to this, I think. For example, "Honey, don't be mad. I didn't know that putting a pinball machine in the dining room would be a problem" is probably a stretch.)

You can't completely eliminate this, but you can do some things differently along the way. Here are a few thoughts:

Involve more groups than you think are necessary to cover a project – Oh how I wish the Exchange Server department would've checked with the Desktop Virtualization people BEFORE they moved to Office 365!

They probably just thought "Outlook is Outlook" and moved right along. As you begin a new project, reach out to all the groups affected, on both the IT and end-user sides, to hear about things you might not have considered.

Proof of Concepts is not the same as pilots – just because it worked ok in the lab, or in your department, doesn't mean it works fine in every situation.

The aforementioned Office 365 move is another good example. A pilot program limited to physical desktops likely worked well, but what about your virtual desktops?

Or your RDSH users? Even things that seem simple should be piloted carefully. Scale up deliberately – some problems don't appear during the PoC or pilot phases, especially the ones you don't know to look for in the first place. When it's time to scale up, don't open the faucet all the way and hope for the best.

Don't forget about users – not all systems are user-facing, but for the ones that are make sure you remember that the users have some control over the success or failure of a project.

***"You can ask all the right questions, drink beer and eat pizza with every department, and execute a perfect PoC and pilot, but if the user experience sucks it will look bad on you."*** – Gabe Knuth

Always maintain respect for the people that have to use your app/platform/service. If you do, they'll help you work through any other issues you didn't know to know about.

**"You don't know what you don't know."**

– Socrates

***Submitted by:***

**Name:** Maarten Caus **Country:** Belgium **Job role:** EUC Consultant **Company:** ITQ

www.linkedin.com/in/maartencaus

www.maartencaus.be

@maartencaus

*Note that these are two submissions merged into one.*

**What is Windows 10 Modern Management?**

Employees want to work on their own devices. Some have different devices like a Windows 10 laptop and a tablet. Employees want to be able to work from any place and from any device. Some organizations might require deep control over devices, while others want lighter management that empowers the modern workforce.

Windows 10 offers the flexibility to respond to those changing requirements. Windows 10 is developed to be managed with a mobile device management solution.

I recently did a proof of concept of Windows 10 Modern Management with VMware Unified Endpoint Management at a customer. It was formerly known as VMware AirWatch. Windows 10 Modern Management has evolved a lot over the past 2 years.

**What are the customers' challenges?**

The customer has offices in many different European countries. The head office is in Belgium. All these countries connect for certain applications to the datacenter in Belgium through VPN. The IT department is also located at the head office in Belgium.

The Belgium IT department is responsible for installing, updating and distributing Dell laptops with Windows 10 to employees.
All the Dell laptops are joined to the domain during installation.
Once the laptop is shipped to an employee it's hard to keep track of the device.

Employees don't have to activate their VPN every time to be able to work. So employees can work off and on the domain. Some laptops only connect once a month to the domain.

The IT department has no insights if the laptops have the latest Windows updates installed, what software is installed and which version, or if the Antivirus definitions are up to date. When a laptop is stolen, or has been compromised, there is no way to wipe the company data from the device.

Employees are not local administrators on their laptops. When they need an update of an application they have to call the IT department. Then an IT administrator takes over the laptop and installs the new update.

**How did we solve these challenges?**

Based on the challenges above we concluded the following goals:

- Enrollment of Windows 10 laptops
- Software catalog with Win32 applications
- Windows Update Management
- Set security policies and force encryption
- Manage firmware and driver updates

### Windows 10 enrollment

There are many different ways to enroll a Windows 10 device. For the POC we downloaded and installed the UEM Hub. We registered the email domain for Auto discovery. When a user wants to enroll a device he simply enters his email address, and through Auto discovery the device is enrolled.

### Software catalog with Win32 applications

We created a software catalog with the company's standard applications. This makes it easier for employees because they have now one single pane of glass to install and update their applications. You can also add any application from the Windows Store to the catalog.

So if you want to add Candy Crush to the catalog, you can!
The successful deployment of applications depends on the quality of your package. Always test the deployment before uploading it. You always need to add an uninstall command as well. Quick tip: if you leave the retry interval default it can take a very long time before VMware UEM retries to the install the application again. (Been there, done that.)

### Windows Update Management

You can centrally manage Microsoft Windows Updates from the console from anywhere. You can use the built-in Microsoft Update Branches to approve and install updates. You can assign the different Microsoft Update Branches to different smart groups. For example, Release Windows Insider Build to the IT department and Semi-Annual Channel to all other departments.

**Security policies and encryption**

Security is becoming more and more important as cyberthreats keep growing every year. We can manage many different security settings in a profile like:

- Is the device managed by MDM?
- Firewall Status
- Antivirus Status
- Automatic Updates
- BitLocker Protection: On or Off

You can also set compliance rules if one or more of the security rules are breached, i.e. if the Antivirus is turned of you can send an automatic mail to an employee, informing that the Antivirus is turned off. If after a few days the Antivirus is not turned on again you can set another automatic action to remove access to company resources.

**Firmware and driver updates**

The customers laptops are mostly Dell devices. We can leverage with the Dell Client Command Suite to improve modern management. The integration enabled the customer to:

- Create reports on custom system properties
- Set BIOS attributes like the BIOS Administrator password
- Configure OEM Update settings

## Conclusion

All major vendors like Microsoft, Citrix and VMware are developing and improving Modern Management. Windows Intune, Citrix Endpoint Management and VMware UEM are evolving, and more features are announced each update. Modern management enables IT administrators to manage devices anywhere and anytime. It offers flexibility and efficiency of use to employees. Modern management is evolving fast, so make sure you're on-board.

***Submitted by:***

**Name:** Jack Lee **Country:** Canada **Job role:** Senior Consultant

 @jlee_consulting

It's all about time-management. Never wait till the 11th hour to do your work. Everybody has a busy schedule one way or another. To be successful, you just need to plan ahead.

***Submitted by:***

**Name:** Marcin Policht **Country:** US. **Job role:** IT Engineer and Architect

Learn principles of Cloud design and apply them uniformly regardless of your choice of Cloud provider. Steer away from dependencies on a particular operating system, middleware platform, or application.

Embrace diversity and open source – remember that more than 50% of Azure VMs are running Linux – including those providing software-defined network functionality.

**Sponsored content**

Nutanix enables IT teams to build and operate powerful multi-Cloud architectures. Our Enterprise Cloud OS software melds private, public and distributed Cloud operating environments and provides a single point of control to manage IT infrastructure and applications at any scale.

Nutanix Digital Workspace enables both end-user computing (EUC) on the industry-leading Enterprise Cloud OS software aka EUC on hyperconverged infrastructure (HCI) and Xi Frame Desktop-as-a-Service (DaaS).

Xi Frame is a virtual desktop service offered by Nutanix. The goal of Xi Frame is to securely connect users, apps, and data from anywhere to any device. It's simple because it just works. It delivers positive results fast. And it normalizes excellence in user experience.

Try **Xi Frame** out for free with a Test Drive:

https://fra.me/test-drive

Visit https://nutanix.com/frame for more info about Xi Frame. For a live demo walk-through with our sales specialist, contact us at frame-sales@nutanix.com.

***Submitted by:***

**Name:** Bas van Kaam **Country:** Netherlands **Job role:** Sr. Business Consultant & Cloud Technologist **Company:** Salomon IT

www.linkedin.com/in/basvankaam

www.basvankaam.com

@BasvanKaam

I like Cloud, I like AWS, Azure, and all the others. I particularly like the flexibility Cloud services potentially offer. I have had many discussions (in a good way) with customers, partners, colleagues, peers, and so on about when the Cloud makes the most sense.

I'm a 'whatever fits my customers use case best' kind of guy, that's why I think of Cloud services as a potential solution to my problem or challenge, but that's it – it's no silver bullet.

In fact, when used incorrectly Cloud often introduces new challenges. Having said that, it's obvious that (hybrid) Cloud services, in general, are slowly taking over. It will take some time, sure, but it's an undeniable fact.

Just don't think that by using Cloud services, never mind in which shape or form, all your troubles will magically disappear. Some might; not all, though.

Finally, Cloud is often referred to as, well... Cloud. Without specifying what type or sort of Cloud service or services is/are being used, or considered.

This makes discussions around what works and what doesn't extremely difficult. My advice would be to first specify the type of services you are dealing with, or are interested in, before anything else. Cloud computing can make life a lot easier, but it can also make things overly complex if you're not careful.

***Submitted by:***

**Name:** Hans Kraaijeveld **Country:** Netherlands **Job role:** Mobility Consultant **Company:** Fondo

www.linkedin.com/in/jpkraaijeveld

www.plonius.com

@hanskraaijeveld

Fundamental to project delivery (yes, also anything Cloud-related) is documentation. Inventory, design, installation, configuration, operational procedures, user manuals... you name it. Everyone knows this, but why oh why do we so often find ourselves in situations in which documentation is incomplete, incorrect or even untraceable?

It starts at the beginning, with the sales process. Take into account that documentation takes time! If you do not plan for it to happen, it WILL not happen. Be strict about it and make it a clear deliverable. Both to yourself, the project and the customer alike, it should be clear as to what it should accomplish.

***"The guy who knows about computers is the last person you want to have creating documentation for people who don't understand computers."***
– Adam Osborne

It has a lot of advantages to do so. You will be able to troubleshoot faster and easier, you can perform upgrades much quicker and you can share the knowledge with any new colleague or project member. It will save you time in the future, so please... invest the time. Make your own templates or use the ones provided by either your company or supplier: they tend to have them, so ask! Do yourself, your company, your colleagues and your customers this favor, and document!!

***Submitted by:***

**Name:** Sacha Thomet **Country:** Switzerland **Job role:** System Engineer **Company:** Die Mobiliar

www.linkedin.com/in/sachathomet

www.sachathomet.ch

@sacha81

I noticed first, especially in the country where I live, Switzerland, nearly nobody had the courage to move anything to the Cloud. Cloud was another word for "evil". Many companies hide themselves behind the legislation for banks and some other industries: they are not allowed to save data outside Switzerland.

Now, in the last two years I've seen a big change: a lot of companies try now to adopt the Cloud, some as fast as possible and without enough planning and absolutely precipitously.

Honestly, I think it's a really bad idea, to do that now for "prestige reasons". Just to say, ok we are now also going the Cloud-way, we are also the cool kids. I see some similarities to the "SBC-Hype" some years ago.

It really makes sense to process the data where the data is. As an example, why use an image processing application on a terminal server to change an image on a workstation, where the image is saved on and where the power of the computer is high enough?

So today I see some companies which try to put workloads in the Cloud, but data remains on-prem for "security reasons" ... in my opinion this just makes no sense. In most cases it makes sense to process the data where the data are. And this doesn't mean keep all on-prem or put all in the Cloud. it means to Cloud for the right part – maybe it's all, maybe it's nothing.

I believe technically most Cloud providers know what they do, and they can do it even better than most companies. The real problem is not the Cloud provider who can't handle the risks, it's the Cloud customer who is perhaps not (yet) aware how he has to configure what ...

***Submitted by:***

**Name:** Rasmus Raun-Nielsen **Country:** Denmark **Job role:** Sr. System Consultant **Company:** Conecto A/S

 www.linkedin.com/in/rasmus-raun-nielsen-6592726

 @RBRConecto

GPU's

The Cloud gives you flexibility so why not try out those GPUs?

Starting with the cons:

Pricing...

At the right price level, though, I expect all will choose GPU-enabled VM instances for their EUC, because the benefits are plenty:

CPU offloading:

- Win10 requires a DirectX 9-based graphics card. If a physical GPU is not present, the Hypervisor tricks the VM-instances to believe that a GPU is present, but under the covers it is emulated in software and executed on the CPU. This is with a limited graphical feature set as opposed to a real GPU resource, and obviously it costs valuable CPU cycles.
- Server 2016 has DirectX built in as well

- Graphics rendering is accelerated by the GPU, so when users are going to utilize multi-monitor with large resolutions you do not get as much of a performance hit on the CPU resources
- Decoding of video can be done on the GPU, freeing CPU resources to other tasks
- Encoding to remoting protocols can be done on the GPU, freeing CPU resources to other tasks – this means you may be able to compress data even further without the significant performance hit. For instance, H.265 is only available with GPU acceleration, as the CPU otherwise would be too overloaded.

Consistent user experience:

- As the GPU is doing the above tasks, the user experience is not affected as much by a fluctuating CPU resource consumption
- All applications as well as the OS work as intended
- All applications can be run with their full feature set in the Cloud EUC environment when all expected resources are available and not being emulated by software.
- GPU progress is lightning-fast and new architectures have new features. Choosing GPUs in the Cloud makes it possible to try out different GPUs in a jiffy.

***Submitted by:***

**Name:** Frank Recker **Country:** Germany **Job role:** IT Architect

www.linkedin.com/in/frank-recker-admincafe

www.admincafe.de

@infofrs

3D VDI Desktops in the Cloud? Good or bad choice?

Many vendors like VMware, Citrix, Nutanix, etc. are offering new options to deliver extreme workload-heavy machines for delivery out of the Cloud. To take the right decision you should be able to answer some questions.

Pros:

- Easy to use recommended?
- Small load times needed?
- Pay per use and not spending much in hardware and people?
- No updates if a vendor published a new version?

Cons:

- Have workloads like 3D Construction Layers needed to upload (CATIA, Siemens, etc.)?
- Extreme secure data like medical stuff in use?
- High latencies between users and VM Portal?
- Other national regulations in focus and use?

There are a scenarios for 3D Desktops in the Cloud. But the main focus in Construction, Medical and Secure Business Scenarios will not be able to use these options.

***Submitted by:***

**Name:** Thomas Poppelgaard **Country:** Denmark **Job role:** Independent Consultant **Company:** Poppelgaard.com

in www.linkedin.com/in/thomaspoppelgaard

www.poppelgaard.com

@_POPPELGAARD

Virtual Reality is evolving fast and makes companies design faster and better products and allows real-time collaboration with min. travel effort. Companies can with Virtual Reality train faster employees.

The big challenge with Virtual Reality in the end-user computing world is that the compute is some of the highest a user can get, having the biggest CPU, GPU, storage and it all has to be rendered at 120FPS down to a headset with 90FPS.

How do you take this complicated workload and put it into a remote protocol and stream it? Citrix HDX can do this today combined with IGEL delivering and end-to-end enterprise solution. NVIDIA also showed at their NVIDIA GTC that they have developed their own RemoteVR solution, so RemoteVR is now real and is here: watch this space.

**"Virtual Reality was once the dream of science fiction. But the Internet was also once a dream and so were computers and smartphones."** – Mark Zuckerberg

# Design principles

***Submitted by:***

**Name:** Rutger de Boer **Country:** Netherlands **Company:** DTX B.V.

www.dtx.nl

When deploying licenses to users, make sure you don't use the same mechanism to distribute the license and the feature. Use different rules for each. A lot of times you will want to up- or downgrade users' licenses based on specific features the users are using (or have stopped using).

Also, your SaaS provider is going to change their license offering and add/remove features from licenses down the line. Decoupling function/feature from licensing will create full flexibility to create any set of services.

**"In the event of nuclear war, the only things to survive will be cockroaches, Twinkies, and Windows apps."** – Shawn Bass

A good Cloud architecture relies on well-established Identity Management. Make sure your identity management is well structured and is easy to understand for the workforce. Regular users are easy but what about the specials?

Hospitals use COWs (Computer On Wheels), steel plants use shift workers with color codes that rotate shifts but need the same profile. How do you define those? There is no right or wrong, but make sure you grasp each and every use case at a client before creating an identity management solution. Because if you take short cuts here it will bite you in the ass later!

***Submitted by:***

**Name:** Dennis Span **Country:** Austria

www.at.linkedin.com/in/dennis-span-3460155b

www.dennisspan.com

@dennisspan

Many organizations today are moving their on-premises production systems (servers) to the Cloud, or at least parts of them. This means that your systems are divided between your on-premises datacenter and the datacenter of the Cloud provider. And this may very well be a permanent situation, unless you plan to migrate all of your systems to the Cloud.

Before migrating to the Cloud, make sure you view your current on-premises infrastructure holistically. What I am getting at is that some components in your infrastructure need to be in close proximity to each other in order to work and perform at their highest level. Moving only some of these components to the Cloud means that there will be an increased latency between the components in the on-premises datacenter and those in the Cloud datacenter (depending on the physical distance).

This may have a negative impact on the overall performance (and subsequently in user satisfaction) of the system. For example, when moving your Citrix workers to the Cloud, you need to take into account the components that the Citrix Worker depends on, such as the user profile, the home drive and the backend systems that are used by your client/server applications.

To achieve the highest performance, you want to minimize the latency between these various components. For this reason, you may have to move more components to the Cloud than you planned initially.

***Submitted by:***

**Name:** Martin Therkelsen **Country:** Denmark **Job role:** Solutions Architect **Company:** Conecto

www.linkedin.com/in/martin-therkelsen-9739895

www.citrixlab.dk

@Mracket

When you do Cloud deployments my best advice is to spend a fair amount of time designing the solution. One of the most important points to Cloud deployments is the network and high availability design.

Network design needs to be thought through since it can be hard to change when the solution is fully deployed. Based on what I have seen, a lot of people forget to design their network in the Cloud as they would do on-premises.

Elements like firewalls and firewall rules are not implemented when using a Cloud solution, so the customers end up with a solution that is very insecure. If you have implemented such a solution the best thing to do is go back to the drawing board and do proper designing and document all the firewall rules needed; after that you can do the implementation. High availability design needs the same amount of planning since you need to take the Cloud provider SLA into account and ensure that all roles are deployed according to Cloud vendor requirements.

If we take Microsoft Azure as an example you can only get an SLA of 99.95% if you use availability sets to ensure virtual machines and load balancers are placed in different update groups, and failure groups and this way Microsoft guarantees the uptime. This is also a point that I have seen a lot of people forget, and as with networks the best advice is to go back to the design phase and do proper designing and then implement that from the bottom up.

***Submitted by:***

**Name:** Ton de Vreede **Country:** Netherlands **Job role:** Freelance Consultant

www.linkedin.com/in/theartvark

www.citrixlab.dk

 @WillCode4Cheese

**Don't sweat too much about your data in the Cloud.**

Many people are nervous about storing their data in the Cloud. Yes, Cloud platforms are high-profile targets for nefarious ne'er-do-wells. Yes, you no longer have a suitcase with backup tapes handcuffed to your wrist. And yes, not all data is suitable (or legal) to store in the Cloud.

*Do* think about what you are storing there, *do* follow the legal requirements for storing your data. But remember that Cloud platforms have hundreds of highly skilled engineers working on security and data protection.

More than any company I have ever worked for could afford. Security is a full-time job and is often still overlooked (especially in smaller sites). And many times a security officer would be happy to have a professional framework in place they can work with instead of having to chase after every detail.

**Keep your data next to your data-munchers**

It may seem obvious but it's a well-known rule that is too often ignored: keep your data close to your processing.

"Yeah, we have too much data. So we are putting it in the Cloud. But our application servers are 'special' so we will keep them here. Hybrid rulez, right?"

True. For a low transaction count application. For your batch test that will send a few hundred sequential queries to the database. And then when you go to production and your up-link gets hit with thousands of transactions every second, simultaneously, latency could hit you. Hard.

Often it is not the bandwidth but the added latency that will really slow down processing. Nothing is impossible: test well, your mileage may vary. Just make sure you really stress-test the application to death.

*On the other hand, if you are running out of space keeping the data local but storing all your back-ups in the Cloud may be a good compromise.*

***"Ten years ago, Amazon found that every 100ms of latency cost them 1% in sales. Google found an extra .5 seconds in search page generation time dropped traffic by 20%. A broker could lose $4 million in revenues per millisecond if their electronic trading platform is 5 milliseconds behind the competition."***

– Nati Shalom @BetaNews

***Submitted by:***

**Name:** Aaron Parker **Country:** Australia **Job role:** Solution Architect **Company:** Insentra

www.linkedin.com/in/aaronedwardparker

www.stealthpuppy.com

@stealthpuppy

The design document is dead. Long live the design document!

In a world with Cloud-based solutions often being the default, continuous integration and monthly or even weekly releases, creating detailed design documents for an infrastructure project is not viable. Focus instead on ensuring that a project is driven by high-level design documents that capture business and technical requirements and clearly state the project goals that align with those requirements.

Look for alternative means to capture detailed design artefacts such as automating deployments with code, automatically capturing environment details as they are built, or even tracking details or changes in something as simple as a spreadsheet. Don't get caught in the weeds at the expense of being able to pivot quickly to take advantage of new features as they are delivered.

***Submitted by**:*

**Name:** DJ Eshelman **Country:** US. **Company:** Eshelman Enterprises

www.linkedin.com/in/djeshelman

www.ctxpro.com

@TheCitrixCoach

A few more tips from DJ. *Check out his Top 3 Citrix Mistakes – How to Be a #CitrixHero! Free ebook on his website.*

**Cloud Resources Aren't Like Local Resources**

Another myth is that deploying resource VMs to a public Cloud will be faster or perform better. I have rarely, if ever, found this to be true. You must approach the Cloud with different design principles than on-prem, especially in terms of CPU and storage.

This is because they weren't generally built with interactive OS sessions in mind. What is true about how CPU performs in your local hypervisor is not true in a public Cloud, where you cannot isolate and fine-tune how the VMs perform.

So, your user experience may be much less predictable than you are used to. Depending on the Cloud provider, this really boils down to treating whitepapers and recommendations as just such. Deploy test VMs and have users REALLY use it.

A common mistake with User Acceptance Testing is treating it like validation. Validation verifies functionality.

UAT should include performance expectations. Make sure you are balancing cost and performance properly for YOUR use case, not what the whitepapers say. Utilize memory-based disk caching as much as you can. Again, you are sharing a massive pool of resources and relying on the Cloud provider for performance.

So, take the in-the-moment performance out the disk equation as much as is practical. For a desktop OS, even a small 64 MB cache can make a big difference. Hopefully it goes without saying that keeping web browsers and programs under control is more important in the Cloud, not less.

***"Remember – a change of premises does not solve problems. If you aren't managing resources well in your datacenter, the problems only get worse in the Cloud."*** – DJ Eshelman

**Busting Maintenance Myths**

A common myth with Citrix Cloud is that "you'll spend less time maintaining servers" means "I don't have to maintain servers!" The truth is that while it is significantly *easier*, and you won't have to do upgrades to the Citrix Control mechanism… connectors and resource VMs still need to be maintained regularly. By YOU.

While the *Citrix* software on the connectors will update occasionally, you must maintain Microsoft updates on those servers, for example. They are still servers in your infrastructure and must be maintained as such. The good news is that back-ups and replication are probably not needed! Back up your master images and you're ready! New connectors deploy rapidly and they do not store retrievable information.

For Resource VMs – *the VDA does not update automatically*. You must regularly download updates to VDA, WEM and any other Citrix software and other control software. The good news is that you don't *have* to match VDA versions with your current 'canary' version in the Citrix Cloud. That said, in order to take advantage of new *features* and policy updates your VDAs must exceed the release with those features.

You may in some circumstances also need to update the Machine Catalog version (type) with the updated VDA to take advantage of certain management features.

Many organizations have made the mistake of thinking going to Citrix Cloud will mean they no longer have to maintain Citrix Administration staff. In some cases, I have seen *more* staff required as adoption increases and more delivery groups are deployed.

***Submitted by:***

**Name:** Steve Noel **Country:** US. **Job role:** Citrix Consultant

www.linkedin.com/in/snoel

www.verticalagetechnologies.com

@Steve_Noel

There are 100 different ways to skin a cat. Designing Cloud-based Citrix environments is no different. There are many different variables and use cases.

Here is one way to skin this cat 'AWS'-style, based on:

*EC2 Machines:*
2x Delivery Controllers
2x NetScaler ADC (Standalone build)
2x Storefront
1x SQL Server
20x VDAs

1. Place half the Infrastructure and VDA machines in one 'Availability Zone' and put the other half in a different 'Availability Zone'. This will help prepare you in case there are certain types of failures.
2. Use Amazon Route 53 to intelligently send users to your NetScaler Gateway in a primary/secondary fashion.
3. Use Elastic Load Balancer for your storefront servers in an active/active fashion. Don't forget to update your internal DNS accordingly.
4. Try to shut down your VDA machines when they are not in use. Citrix Smart Scale (now AutoScale) can help with this. If you don't have the license required for this feature, PowerShell can also be your friend.
5. Don't forget, Citrix Cloud can help you with the heavy lifting by removing all the Citrix/SQL infrastructure EC2Instances.

**"Line-of-business leaders everywhere are bypassing IT departments to get applications from the Cloud (also known as Software-as-a-Service, or SaaS) and paying for them like they would a magazine subscription. And when the service is no longer required, they can cancel that subscription with no equipment left unused in the corner."** – Daryl Plummer

***Submitted by:***

**Name:** Edwin Houben **Country:** Netherlands **Job role:** Sr. Solutions Architect **Company:** ConoScenza

in www.linkedin.com/in/edwinhouben

www.edwinhouben.com

@EHouben

My top 5:

**Think Adaptive and Elastic**

A good Cloud architecture should be designed to support growth of users, traffic, or data size with no performance penalty. It scales linear when and where an additional resource is added or needed. Cloud solutions need to be able to adapt and proportionally serve additional loads.

**Treat servers as disposable resources**

The biggest advantage of Cloud computing is that you can treat your servers as disposable resources instead of fixed components. Resources should always be consistent and thoroughly tested.

**Automate, Automate, Automate**

Unlike traditional IT infrastructure, Cloud enables automation of a number of events, improving both your system's stability and the efficiency of your organization.

**Implement loose coupling**

IT systems should ideally be designed in a way that reduces interdependencies. Your components need to be loosely coupled to avoid changes or failure in one of the components from affecting others.

**KISS (Keep It Simple, Stupid)**

If it sounds difficult, it probably is. To get a simpler solution, step back and try to redesign the solution in a simpler manner.

***Submitted by:***

**Name:** Danny van Dam **Country:** Netherlands **Job role:** Freelance Infrastructure/Cloud/Workspace Architect/Consultant **Company:** DAM IT Consultancy

www.linkedin.com/in/dnyvandam

www.dannyvandam.net

@dnyvandam

In the Cloud focus on fast cores with a higher speed instead of many cores on a lower speed for (multi-session) desktop workloads. It can be tempting to select a VM type with too much core and/or too much memory for a high cost.

> **"DOS is fundamental for Windows, and Windows will be the fundament for Microsoft Azure." – This quote reminds me of how fast we are going (and some of you already did) to leverage Azure Cloud Platform Services."** – Christiaan Brinkhoff

***Submitted by:***

**Name:** James Kindon: Australia **Job role:** Consultant **Company:** Insentra

www.linkedin.com/in/jkindon

www.jkindon.com

 @James_Kindon

When designing for solutions running on public Cloud infrastructure, it can be easy to miss platform- or vendor-specific limits which will have huge impact on your design.

For example, in a Citrix Cloud design with workloads running on Azure, understanding limits from Azure such as API calls, Managed Disks, Resource Group sizing, etc. will all affect what and how you design.

Furthermore, understanding which limitations the Citrix backend providers are hard-coded against will in turn play a part in your design output. Many soft limits from Microsoft can be raised on a per subscription basis; however, some components are hard-coded in the Citrix code which is not aware of individual exemptions.

Rule of thumb will of course to design against the lowest common limitation. A pod architecture design when doing mass workloads in Azure can be beneficial for scale and supportability, even if it does introduce complexity and operational overhead.

***Submitted by:***

**Name:** Jan Hendrik Meier **Country:** Germany **Job role:** Senior Systems Engineer **Company:** Citrix

www.linkedin.com/in/jhmeier

www.jhmeier.com

@jhmeier

**Don't forget the Data and Application connections**

I am regularly involved in discussions about moving VDI / SBC workload to the Cloud. When you think about moving these workloads to the Cloud there are a lot of things to discuss: Is it better to stay with SBC, move to VDI or the other way round? Can we power off the machines to save money, as always running machines costs a lot of money – except you decide to take the "flat rate" options?

There are several other points in this area where you should have a look at when migrating your SBC / VDI workload to the Cloud. But there is one thing which from my point of view is often underestimated:

Where are the application data, documents and user data hosted? Which connections does an application need? If you just move the SBC / VDI workers to the Cloud, install the applications on them like before, create a VPN connection to the Cloud and then the start the application, it suddenly has a higher latency to its backend systems.

This often results in applications reacting slower or even to hang, as they must wait for their backend systems. For the user this is painful as he cannot work as before. Instead he has to wait for the application to react.

So, he will directly dislike the new system and tell everyone that he wants to go back to the old on-prem VDI / SBC. The other thing is that applications often have interfaces to other internal systems. If you now move the application data to the Cloud you need to make sure these interfaces are still working.

Other systems that you never heard about before might be using an interface to your ERP application and suddenly stop working as they cannot connect to the application data any longer – this might lead to critical business outtakes when suddenly something in the production is not working any longer.

Who has not seen a production-relevant application just running for more than ten years and having dozens of interfaces to other applications inside the company?

The other point is the document itself. When it takes the users much longer than before to open a simple document this will also make them feel uncomfortable with the Cloud solution.

Also, you need to think about the user profiles. When you don't store them on a server in the Cloud nearby to the workers, logging on will take longer – not good for the user experience.

To sum it up: When you think about moving SBC / VDI workload (not management infrastructure) to the Cloud do not forget to have a deeper look at the applications, the application databases and the user interfaces. Otherwise you will be extremely quickly moving everything back to on-prem.

***Submitted by:***

**Name:** Igor van der Burgh **Country:** Netherlands **Job role:** Sr. Consultant Citrix Professional Services **Company:** Citrix

www.linkedin.com/in/igor-van-der-burgh-5284947

www.vanderburgh.it

@Igor_vd_burgh

Remember, Citrix Cloud licenses are allocated by OrgID; therefore, a test “site” usually becomes a test “zone”. This should also be considered with a DR site that becomes a DR zone.

Local Host Cache on the Citrix Connector serves to protect against CVAD service outage, but requires additional RAM and CPU. It also requires an on-prem StoreFront environment.

Cloud Connectors need to be designed reliably. Citrix manages the Cloud Connector but not the local infrastructure. Understand key considerations when deploying Citrix on Azure. Highlight the Citrix and Microsoft tools available to support your project.

An Azure Resource Group can hold no more than 800 managed disks. By default, the Virtual Apps and Desktops Service provisions three disks per machine: OS Disk, Identity Disk and Write Back Cache Disk. The Virtual Apps and Desktops Service will provision no more than 240 machines per Azure Resource Group, leaving a small buffer for future use up to the theoretical 266 machines per Azure Resource Group. See the CTX article below: https://support.citrix.com/article/CTX237504.

My recommendation is to use Azure Managed Disks when provisioning the VDA via MCS to provide a seamless and less time-consuming provisioning process.

***Submitted by:***

**Name:** Mitch Meade **Country:** US. **Job role:** Platform Architect II
**Company:** CloudJumper

www.cloudjumper.com

Idempotent-declarative design allows for greater flexibility, migration and recovery; the customer's environment should be described with a series of idempotent and declarative configuration documents that continuously evaluate for compliance.

***"Anything else is just a service tied to manual labor, which is not Cloud-centric and will fail due to introduced irregularities as well as unsurmountable labor efforts."*** – Mitch Meade

**"Our job is to de-suckify shitty User Experience! Managing expectations, use base-practices, process and the right (new) tools!"**

– Benny & Kristin

***Submitted by:***

**Name:** Saadallah Chebaro **Country:** United Arab Emirates **Job role:** Solutions Architect **Company:** Diyar United Company

in www.linkedin.com/in/saadallah-chebaro-ab768227

 www.diyar.online

 @s_chebaro

A common mistake in consuming IaaS workloads on the Cloud is treating VM's consumed resources CPU/memory in a similar fashion to an on-premises datacenter.

***"Monitor VMs utilization on the Cloud constantly to make sure that all resources are being utilized efficiently as using a pay-as-you-go model means you are charged for the VM size/option regardless of how much CPU/memory is being used within."***
– Saadallah Chebaro

If the VM is under-utilized in terms of CPU/memory, make sure to either move to a different size/option or host more workloads on that VM. Remember that Cloud providers guarantee performance and availability through SLA; thus one need not approach utilization in the same manner as on-premises VMs are treated.

Customers considering moving VDI workloads to the Cloud must ensure that their Cloud vendor of choice has a datacenter preferably within the same zone or at least within the same region. Connectivity to VDI workloads is network sensitive, and high latency introduced by datacenters will negatively affect end-user performance.

***Submitted by:***

**Name:** Tobias Kreidl **Country:** US. **Job role:** Systems Architect
**Company:** Northern Arizona University

in www.linkedin.com/in/tobias-kreidl-7ab249a3

@tkreidl

When choosing servers in the Cloud to host your apps, bigger is always better, right? Well, think again, because – as many others have pointed out – this is not always the case.

Sure, you may get more power for a somewhat lower cost with one big server compared to two smaller or even four much smaller ones, but look more closely at a case where your load varies a lot and you do not need to run all your servers all the time to serve your needs.

With more, smaller servers, you have the granularity to shut one or more of them down when they are not needed, while you may have to keep a whole extra-large server still in operation to make sure you don't run out of resources.

Figuring out ahead of time how many servers you will need to keep running at various times to sustain your load could save you a lot of money if that load varies significantly over the course of a day or even a week.

Work out the numbers ahead of time before you settle on a configuration that will not only get the job done for you, but also likely save you money.

***Submitted by:***

**Name:** Ronnie Hamilton **Country:** Ireland **Job role:** Principal Technical Consultant **Company:** DataSolutions

in www.linkedin.com/in/dsronnie

www.ronnie.ie

@RonnieDOTie

Ronnie's top three

1 – Citrix Cloud is not a platform to run your workloads, it's the place to consume Citrix services.

***"When you have a Cloud-only strategy and don't re-platform your workloads, you are preparing to fail as the cost will be massive. Only use the Cloud when it's the correct platform for your workloads or you re-architect using Cloud services."***
– Ronnie Hamilton

3 – It can be difficult to control costs in the Cloud when various business units are involved, Shadow IT can be at play and various accounts with access to your internal network. This can lead to compliance and security issues: there are various products out that can review and optimize your Cloud spend.

***Submitted by:***

**Name:** Marcel Kornegoor **Country:** Netherlands **Job role:** DevOps & Cloud Consultant **Company:** AT Computing

www.linkedin.com/in/mkornegoor

www.kornegoor.org

@mckornegoor

Embrace a Cloud mindset

Moving from your current or legacy environment to the Cloud means a lot of things will change. This fact may cause a contradiction: on the one hand there is the urge of using the possibilities of the Cloud. On the other, there is a desire to keep things the way they are.

Sysadmins and management can be stubborn to embrace change, because change stands synonymous with outages, trouble and stress. Going to the Cloud with minimal change is possible.

Simply *lift and shift* your (virtual!) servers to the datacenters of one Cloud provider or another. Although this will technically work, it also means you only leverage about 1% of the potential of the Cloud. 1% is actually an optimistic number.

The lift-and-shift scenario makes the Cloud an expensive new hosting solution for your servers, without providing you with a lot of new possibilities.

To increase *bang for the buck*, it's wise to look at the Cloud as a green field. Do you really need to build and manage your databases from bare metal or does an *off the shelf* PaaS solution meet your requirements? Are you a hosting and IT infrastructure specialist, or more focused on applications and usage of IT systems?

If the answer is the latter, be thankful you no longer need to worry about swapping hard disks or making your cluster work properly. Whatever you do: grasp thorough knowledge of the Cloud before you start to migrate. Unleashing the true power of the Cloud requires you to embrace a Cloud mindset.

***"The lift-and-shift scenario makes the Cloud an expensive new hosting solution for your servers, without providing you with a lot of new possibilities."*** – Marcel Kornegoor

***Submitted by:***

**Name:** Sarah Lean **Country:** Great Britain **Job role:** Cloud Solution Architect **Company:** Microsoft

in www.in.linkedin.com/in/sazlean

www.techielass.com

@Techielass

If you are an Infrastructure person, a traditional server hugger, please don't be scared to give things like coding, DevOps, Infrastructure as Code, etc. a try.

These things aren't just for the Devs. Through away that mindset and start getting familiar with things like Git, Visual Studio Code and see what you can create, you'll be surprised!

***Submitted by:***

**Name:** Anton van Pelt & Patrick van den Born **Country:** Netherlands **Job role:** Senior Consultant, **Company:** PQR

www.linkedin.com/in/antonvanpelt

www.linkedin.com/in/patrick-van-den-born-2b3567a

www.antonvanpelt.com

www.patrickvandenborn.blogspot.nl

@AntonvanPelt

@pvdnborn

Last year we've deployed some Citrix Virtual Apps and Desktop solutions on Azure. In this article we want to share things we've learned during these projects.

An interesting use case is one of our customers needed flexible capacity for their primary business. A public Cloud like Microsoft Azure gives them the flexibility to temporarily spin up more resources when needed for a short period.

At the moment they are gaining advantage over their competitors and are winning contracts due to their low time to market offering. Since the use of Azure they are able to set up a new office in a very short period. They just need office space with an internet connection, bring in Stratodesk Thin Clients and power-on additional desktops in the Cloud. They can start working for their customers in a very short time.

**Citrix on Azure**

During our projects we've learned that when deploying a Citrix Virtual Apps and Desktops Workload on Azure:

- There is no SQL PaaS support for the Citrix Virtual Apps and Desktops delivery controller. You need to deploy a full-blown SQL-installation in an IaaS Virtual machine on Azure.
- When deploying Windows 10 Enterprise, you will need a Microsoft Enterprise Agreement.
- Citrix Virtual Apps and Desktops doesn't support the Azure Classic Portal: don't use it!
- Use managed disks for your Citrix workers in Azure because:
    - Image deployment and machine provisioning are faster.
    - Image deployment and machine provisioning are more stable.
- Managed disk support for MCS-provisioned virtual machines is introduced in Citrix XenDesktop 7.17 (former name of Virtual Apps and Desktops).
    - Available in Current Release versions of Citrix Virtual Apps and Desktops.
    - Available in Citrix Virtual Apps and Desktops services in Citrix Cloud.
    - Not available in the Long-Term Service Release of Citrix XenDesktop 7.15.
- Citrix Machine Creation Services will remove the image disk and virtual machine from Azure when a worker is powered off by the delivery controller. This will save you money when a worker is not used.
- It can take up to 7 minutes to power-on a Machine Creation Services-provisioned virtual machine on Azure. During power-on, Machine Creation Services will reprovision the virtual machine on the platform.
- When deploying persistent Citrix workers on Azure, an identity disk of 1GiB per worker is deployed on Azure.
    - Citrix Machine Creation Services remain an identity disk per machine in your Machine Catalog.

On Azure this identity disk is of the same storage type as defined for the Machine Catalog and 1GiB in size.

    - Deploying a non-persistent Machine Catalog on Premium SSD will cost you approximately $4 per Identity disk per month (Azure West Europe).
    - Citrix Product Management is already aware of this and is working on a solution. In the meantime, you can, however, change the identity disk from premium SSD to standard HHD. Jane Cassell wrote an article on this; you can find it here: https://bit.ly/2WGeA1y.
- You can use Citrix Smart Scale to scale your Virtual Apps and Desktop workers on public Clouds. It will save you money!
- Smart Scaling is only available for Citrix Cloud CVAD or Citrix CVAD Premium with CSS customers
- Citrix Smart Scale feature is announced deprecated per 31-05-2019. Citrix adjusted this date three times, so we expect there will be a next generation of Citrix Smart Scale
- Citrix Smart Scale can be used with VDI and session hosts.

## Citrix on Azure common practices

During our Citrix on Azure projects, we found the following common practices for deploying Citrix workloads on Azure:

- Adjust registration timers for the Citrix Broker Service to avoid registration failures of your VDAs. We've experienced registration failures when using VDI workers on Azure.
    - CTX126704 (Section VDA registrations): https://support.citrix.com/article/CTX126704
        - DesktopServer\MaxLaunchRegistrationDelaySec
        - DesktopServer\ExtraSpinUpTimeSecs

        - DesktopServer\MaxSessionEstablishmentTimeSecs
- In a 1-on-1 VDI on Azure workload, don't shutdown the virtual machine after logoff. It will deprovision the Citrix Worker, and spinning up a new one will take another 7 minutes.
    - Set-BrokerDesktopGroup -Name "DeliveryGroupName" -ShutdownDesktopAfterUse $false
- When using Citrix Smart Scale with an on-premises deployment. Disable the power management of the delivery controller. Citrix Smart Scale will start and stop the virtual machines. Citrix power management will interference with Smart Scale.

```
Add-PSSnapin *Citrix*
Set-BrokerDesktopGroup -Name * -
AutomaticPowerOnForAssigned $False
Set-BrokerDesktopGroup -Name * -
AutomaticPowerOnForAssignedDuringPeak $False
Set-BrokerDesktopGroup -Name * -OffPeakBufferSizePercent
0
Set-BrokerDesktopGroup -Name * -PeakBufferSizePercent 0
Set-BrokerPowerTimeScheme -name * -PoolSize (1..24 | %{ -1
} ) -PoolUsingPercentage 0
```

- Use Citrix Smart Scale power-off delay setting to delay the shutdown and virtual machine removal.
    - If a user decides to login after logoff, the virtual machine is instantly available.
    - If no user is getting back to the Citrix Worker after the delay timer, the virtual machine will be powered off by Smart Scale to prevent IaaS costs.
- When deploying Citrix workers with Machine Creation Services on Premium SSD, move the Identity disks to Standard HHD.

    - This will save you approximately $4 per Citrix Worker per month (Azure West Europe)
- As of March 2019, the Windows 10 Enterprise for Virtual Desktops image is available on Azure. You can use this with Citrix Virtual Apps and Desktops as a multi-session OS. So if you need Windows 10 and your application is working with this new version of Windows, it might be a better option than a 1-on-1 VDI on Azure.
- From a management perspective, it is much better to use Citrix Cloud Virtual Apps and Desktops Services, Citrix Cloud Gateway Services and Citrix Workspace App.
    - Citrix will update the backend for you.
    - Your Citrix backend virtual machines like Microsoft SQL, Deliver Controllers, StoreFront, Citrix ADC and Licensing servers are not needed. You do not have to manage these virtual machines.
    - A deployment of two IaaS virtual machines with Citrix Cloud Connectors is enough.
    -

**"If you don't jump on the new, you don't survive."**

– Satya Nadella

***Submitted by:***

**Name:** Jim Moyle **Country:** Great Britain **Job role:** Technical Evangelist **Company:** Microsoft

www.linkedin.com/in/jimmoyle

www.youtube.com/jimmoyle

@JimMoyle

*'The Cloud is too expensive'* is something I hear a lot. Maybe you say it. This is an incorrect statement, or rather a statement that requires more context.

A better way to put it would be: if I lift and shift my on-premises infrastructure to the Cloud, it will cost me more to run than my current setup. An even better way to put it is: The engineering effort to move to the Cloud and make it cheaper and better than my current setup is too much work and I don't have the time or energy.

When moving to the Cloud, I encourage you to follow the following adage: **No Virtual Machines**. You may have to break apart your existing apps, redesign them to take advantage of PaaS, or replace them entirely with SaaS offerings. You should be looking at new data storage platforms, new identity methods and serverless computing, all this without standing up a single VM.

***"Virtual Machines in the Cloud are the worst of both worlds, don't do it."*** – Jim Moyle

To some people in your organization this will be an anathema, and you probably won't be able to bring them with you as you progress. Look for the people in your organization who are already embracing DevOps practices to help. If you ask for an analysis of how much it will cost you to move to the Cloud and the answer comes back without an eventual reduction in VMs by around 80%, ask someone else.

**Sponsored content**

Goliath Technologies provides IT operations software that enables IT professionals to anticipate, troubleshoot and prevent end-user experience issues regardless of where IT workloads or users are located. This is achieved through end-to-end monitoring from the remote user to the Cloud-hosted applications, infrastructure or desktops. It works by providing the real-time metrics to troubleshoot the issue with corresponding analysis and reports. These document true root cause and include fix actions that can be put in place to permanently resolve the issue.

***"Whether you are using a Virtual Desktop on-premises and using the management plane, like Citrix Cloud or Horizon Cloud, or have it all running in Infrastructure-as-a-Service on Microsoft Azure – you don't want to use all the separate consoles together to monitor the different solutions you are using. This is where the Goliath Performance Monitor can make a huge difference."***

Try it yourself and see how this powerful, purpose-built software will help you anticipate, troubleshoot and prevent end-user issues, regardless of where your end-users, infrastructure or data are located.

Contact us at techinfo@goliathtechnologies.com or call (855) 465-4284 for a free, fully supported 30-day trial.

***Submitted by:***

**Name:** DJ Eshelman **Country:** US. **Company:** Eshelman Enterprises

www.linkedin.com/in/djeshelman

www.ctxpro.com

@TheCitrixCoach

**DJ's top 3**

*Tip 1: Citrix Cloud High Level Tips*

Citrix Cloud is a powerful & scalable way to not have to maintain redundant databases and Control servers. The more you scale, the more the benefit. For example, consider each hub location having a datacenter with Resources. Citrix Cloud allows deployment of the CVAD and WEM services much more rapidly. You really just need 2 connectors per site.

You are only EVER as strong as your weakest point. Unlike traditional controllers, Cloud Connectors often need more CPU, RAM and disk resources as they proxy multiple functionality. Don't be shy giving each connector ½ of your pCPU value as vCPU (e.g. a 12-core processor would get 6 vCPU) and 12-16GB RAM with 100GB storage.

Scalable and easy does NOT excuse bad design or, even worse, not maintaining the connector servers themselves. Take the time that you would be spending maintaining a local database and spend it on fully optimizing your Resource Layer.

Resource Layer (Server & Desktop VDAs) must be fully optimized regardless of their platform location (on-prem, Cloud, etc.). These optimizations should be driven completely by the user needs balanced with the business needs.

*Don't be a Fool, Use the Citrix Optimizer tool!*

Deploy to 10% of the population size and observe carefully if your CPU and RAM configuration meets or exceeds the user need. Only scale when you have selected the correct configuration!

If you don't consider how your resources map to users' needs you will only scale failure.

*Tip 2: Adopt a Services Methodology*

My methodology is as follows: Understand, Plan, Change, Maintain. The process is iterative, functioning in a cycle (where Maintain then feeds back into Understand). At any point in the process you may need to go back to a previous step if risk is identified. Example project: Validated Design.

**Understand**

- Interview business leadership to understand their objectives. What are their priorities? What does success look like to them? (This may be the single most important question you could ask. NEVER ASSUME!)
- Interview representatives of each user group. What devices do they use? What peripherals? What applications do they *really* need? What workarounds do they employ today to get their work done?
- What Access strategy is appropriate for the user and business objectives? In what contexts will they perform work?
- Map the Resource requirements of each use case (where a business priority meets a user to fulfill it). You should have a table of what applications map to each user group and the application requirements (if any noted).

**Plan**

- Create a Conceptual Design to fulfill the Understand phase.
- Plan a POC Deployment and define success criteria.

**Change**

- Deploy the Conceptual Design components
- Add a small number of users and validate the use cases are filled.
- Circle back to the Understand phase and back thru Plan and Change for any unmet requirements
- Once Validated as Best Viable Product (NOT Minimum Viable), Scale to production or Rebuild production

**Maintain**

- Monitor for steady-state.
- Backup and Secure.
- Scale.
- Any deltas or new requirements will trigger a rapid cycle thru the methodology.

Never skip a step in the process because it is a crisis. This will only make things worse!

*Tip 3: Profile Management for the Hybrid Cloud*

Taking a hybrid approach to deploying Virtual Apps & Desktops? A design consideration is maintaining user persona in the Cloud and on-premises. The default 'include all' strategy can quickly grow out of control and become slow and expensive.

- Understand when personal management must persist between your on-prem datacenter(s) & your Cloud instance. If Cloud is just "DR" then you may not need to. If it is a need, identify the specific elements required: e.g. if you are deploying Outlook on-prem with .OST files & your Cloud location is Azure – you don't need an .OST file at all; but there is value in the local contacts, signature, etc. to persist in multiple locations.

- Choose a strategy that will allow you to properly include and exclude these files and settings. For a Hybrid deployment with Citrix Profile Management – exclude by default and only include what will be required. A suggestion for this: with a 'clean' profile have a user perform their functions per app and track what files and folders are created. Then determine which files are required. The time spent here can save huge potential headaches. But it will be a substantial time commitment!
- Fully understand your replication ability. In some cases, a simple solution of replicating an attached-disk solution is best. But if you are replicating files – be very careful, you aren't replicating junk! Looking at you, Google Chrome! But a huge key here is deduplication and being selective about what is replicated.
- For a hybrid Cloud – definitely go 'beyond the box'. Third-party solutions are likely to be your friend. You'll spend less time managing everything I just mentioned!

***Submitted by:***

**Name:** Marius Sandbu **Country:** Norway **Job role:** Cloud Architect **Company:** EVRY

www.msandbu.org

 @msandbu

In the next couple of years, more and more of the virtual infrastructure that we have today running on VMware / Hyper-V / XenServer or virtual infrastructure in the Cloud will be replaced with large container orchestration environments using Kubernetes or some other form of container orchestration.

Container-based environments will provide a lot more flexibility to the development teams and allow them to handle the entire release pipelines using a common set of tools with little involvement from the Operations team.

Moving forward, it will be crucial for us who work in Operations to provide and also to learn the foundation so that the development team can provide and build new services. Also ensuring that security is a core part of that foundation.

***Submitted by:***

**Name:** Jan de Vries **Country:** Netherlands **Job role:** Cloud Solution Architect / Developer **Company:** 4DotNet

 www.linkedin.com/in/jandv

 www.jan-v.nl

 @crmgustaf

For several years, if not decades, we have been developing software as large systems. Most of the time these systems consist of several modules, each doing their own thing, and if you're lucky enough there is a clear separation between these modules.

You might not call it modules, but rather components, services or maybe even a bounded context. Either way, it's functionality which lives inside your processes and hopefully delivers some crucial business value. These processes are deployed to locations either on-premises or in the Cloud.

This will come to an end, sooner rather than later! Every Cloud provider is upping its game with the serverless revolution.

This means, in not too much time, we will not develop our modules inside big processes anymore. We will instead build small 'services' which will only host the core functionality. This functionality will only contain the business logic necessary to add value to the company. All of the plumbing, setup and other cross-cutting concerns will be abstracted away from the regular developer.

This way our developers can focus on adding more value to our customers instead of lots and lots of code. The first phase of this serverless shift is going on right now. Every Cloud provider has its own offering to deliver some serverless compute, also known as Functions-as-a-Service.

By leveraging the native powers of these FaaS offerings you can already start to see the value because a lot of the plumbing logic is handled by the platform runtime.

There is still a lot of functionality missing out of the box, true for each Cloud provider, but this will change over time. As I've said, we've only just started getting our feet wet in the serverless world. In short, I'd say, hop on the serverless bandwagon and make your voice heard while we're evolving the current serverless platform to the next version!

***Submitted by:***

**Name:** Gustaf Westerlund **Country:** Sweden **Job role:** Dynamics 365 Solution Architect, MVP, Founder CRM-Konsulterna
**Company:** CRM – Konsulterna i Sverige AB

www.linkedin.com/in/gustafwesterlund

www.powerplatform.se

@crmgustaf

Cloud computing has some important aspects that I, as a Dynamics 365 Solution Architect, like to emphasize. First of all, not all Clouds are the same. I sometimes hear from customers that they are so happy that they are in the Cloud and then find that they are simply running VMs in the Cloud.

As an architect of a very high-octane SaaS service, I of course see the difference between running a server program installed in a VM and having an SaaS service.

Hence I think it is important to try to constantly have an ambition to constantly refine the level of Cloudiness in the organization's entire meta system or ecosystem. In other words moving up in the chain of on-prem -> IaaS -> PaaS -> SaaS.

Another interesting aspect of Cloud computing I often encounter is that organizations look for different Cloud systems in an attempt to find the best-of-breed and connect them together in a notion that Cloud systems are easy to integrate.

This can of course sometimes be true, if someone has built an out-of-the-box integration or there are adaptors to common integration engines, but I often find that despite this, the utility of having all systems from the same supplier vastly outshines any smaller lack of feature found in any of the subsystems.

Also the birth of many PaaS-level modular components, like Azure Cognitive Services, can be a lot more easily integrated with systems from the same supplier (Microsoft) than from other suppliers.

Hence I think that many organizations should not only tactically choose different SaaS systems to migrate to on a Cloud basis, they also should choose Ecosystems-as-a-Service or Meta-systems-as-a-Service that best fits their needs.

Weighing in factors like office collaboration, business systems, ease of integration with common tools, ease of finding talented developers for custom development, ability to extend with modular components, inter-system integration costs and maintenance costs.

Final word is, Cloud computing is a long-term strategic transition to enable digital transformation in a more rapid manner than the option of choosing on-prem. It is important to make the right choices and set the right strategic plans.

**"The last ten years of IT have been about changing the way people work. The next ten years of it will be about transforming your business."** – Aaron Levie

***Submitted by:***

**Name:** Marcel Kornegoor **Country:** Netherlands **Job role:** DevOps & Cloud Consultant **Company:** AT Computing

www.linkedin.com/in/mkornegoor

www.kornegoor.org

@mckornegoor

APIs are your friends, but they are not always friendly.

Make sure you master the use of APIs. This way you will be able to tie various applications, data sources, functionality and services together fast and secure. Although it may be hard at first, using APIs eventually will save a lot of time and prevent you from inventing your own wheel over and over again.

When you consider yourself skilled in using APIs, start thinking about writing an API for your own application or platform. Look at yourself as a service provider and make sure other teams can easily interact with your service. Creating an API is an important step towards self-service and facilitates a high level of automation.

One of the prime examples of API use is Google. They even choose to write custom APIs for third-party software if the API it comes with does not live up to their standards. Although this requires a lot of effort, the possibilities a good API creates will earn itself back over time.*

For developers, working with APIs might sound like just another day at the office. Could be, but please do not underestimate it. Every API has its unique properties and oddities. Particularly working with APIs that are built with OAuth 2.0 and tokens might be a pickle. For sysadmins, working with APIs can be really challenging.

You need to have basic or maybe even advanced knowledge of programming and thorough scripting skills are absolutely required to professionally use an API.

There are some points of attention you should be aware of when you start your API journey. First and foremost: think about security. With an API, you are letting your application exchange data with another application. This requires careful handling of not only the data itself, but also things like key pairs, tokens, secrets or other forms of credentials.

Make sure you know what you are doing with them. Also make sure you always use transport encryption (e.g. with TLS). This prevents data that travels from one datacenter to another via some internet connection from being intercepted.

Besides security, documentation is of the essence. When you decide to create your own API, make sure the corresponding documentation is mature. This not only prevents using the API from going wrong, but also reduces the number of questions you get from your API users. This helps the self-service concept and ensures you can focus on your actual work instead of mutating into an API service desk.

Last, but not least: make sure you are always aware of the API version. Since the owner of the API may periodically update it, functionality may differ depending on the version. Although it is a common practice for APIs to be backward compatible, this sometimes is not the case.

* https://landing.google.com/sre/sre-book/chapters/automation-at-google/

***Submitted by:***

**Name:** Aman Sharma **Country:** Canada **Job role:** Principal Technical Consultant **Company:** Green House Data

www.linkedin.com/in/20aman?originalSubdomain=ca

www.harvestingclouds.com

@20aman

When you are programming anything related to the Cloud (Microsoft Azure or AWS or any other Cloud) you will have different options to achieve the end result. You will be interacting with the Cloud APIs in one way or another.

E.g. You want to automate shutdown or start of the virtual machines in the Cloud, based on a schedule. You can either write a PowerShell script or author a command line-based script or code around that Cloud provider's SDK or interact directly with the REST APIs. As a best practice, your first choice should always be coding directly to the REST APIs.

The biggest benefit that you get with this approach is that you remove your dependency on installing a PowerShell module or SDK on the machine. The REST protocol is natively supported in almost all the platforms and it frees you from any dependencies. This means less management overhead during the deployment or during the life cycle of the application.

This is an industry standard which is available in almost all environments, and therefore also saves you the trouble of setting up complex rules in the firewall. From the performance perspective, you gain an advantage as well (although very small) as there is no wrapper on the APIs now. Also, it ensures that you are building on a model which is supported on all platforms.

This best practice will ensure that your application is forward compatible to any changes with the API with minimal changes in the code. Therefore I recommend that you should always try and explore REST API as your first choice for any customizations or programming around the Cloud technologies.

***Submitted by:***

**Name:** Neil McLoughlin **Country:** Great Britain **Job role:** Citrix Consultant **Company:** Nationwide Building Society

 www.linkedin.com/in/neilmcloughlin

 www.virtualmanc.co.uk

 @virtualmanc

Remember why we implement Citrix in the first place

Before VDI was even a thing traditional IT infrastructure consisted of a datacenter full of servers with the users connecting their front-end clients to backend services over slow and unreliable ISDN WAN links located in different branches throughout the country or even different countries. The user experience wasn't great.

Then this wonderful thing called Citrix came along which enabled us to connect to our servers directly in the datacenter. Now we were accessing everything over a 1gbps connection instead of a 128k ISDN link. Happy users ☺

The evolution of Cloud Computing has given us more options and locations to deploy resources than we have ever had before. It seems like every quarter there are more and more regions appearing in Azure, AWS & Google Cloud. Azure currently has 54 regions available in 140 countries, and I am sure this will continue to increase. But this introduces a new problem.

One application could be Azure-hosted in the US, another could be on-premises-hosted in Holland and my user data could be sitting in Google Cloud in France. Oh, and my VDI desktop is sitting in Japan West and I am accessing it from my home in the UK (This is an extreme example, I know!)

As I type this here are some latency stats from some Azure regions accessed from the UK. My best is 66ms and the worst is 585ms. Users and applications are going to notice 585ms latency.

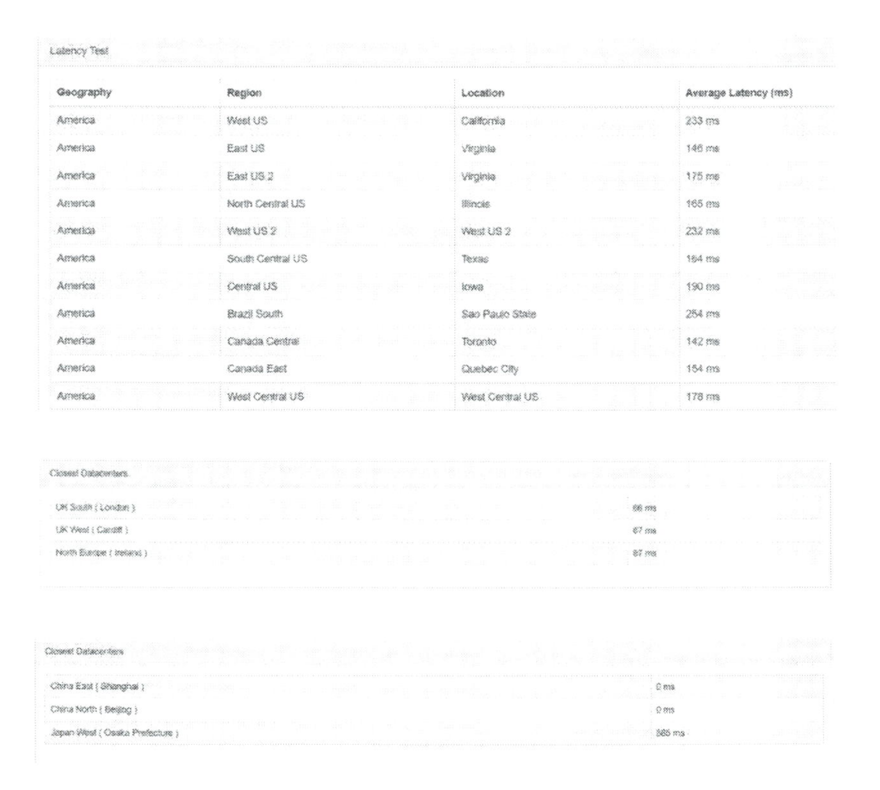

Latency Test

| Geography | Region | Location | Average Latency (ms) |
|---|---|---|---|
| America | West US | California | 233 ms |
| America | East US | Virginia | 146 ms |
| America | East US 2 | Virginia | 175 ms |
| America | North Central US | Illinois | 165 ms |
| America | West US 2 | West US 2 | 232 ms |
| America | South Central US | Texas | 184 ms |
| America | Central US | Iowa | 190 ms |
| America | Brazil South | Sao Paulo State | 254 ms |
| America | Canada Central | Toronto | 142 ms |
| America | Canada East | Quebec City | 154 ms |
| America | West Central US | West Central US | 178 ms |

Closest Datacenters

| | |
|---|---|
| UK South ( London ) | 66 ms |
| UK West ( Cardiff ) | 67 ms |
| North Europe ( Ireland ) | 87 ms |

Closest Datacenters

| | |
|---|---|
| China East ( Shanghai ) | 0 ms |
| China North ( Beijing ) | 0 ms |
| Japan West ( Osaka Prefecture ) | 585 ms |

Now the connection to my VDI Desktop isn't great and the application response times are poor, and the general user experience is rubbish.

So, my top tip is, if exploring Desktop-as-a-Service or sticking your applications or VDI Desktops in the Cloud, please be mindful of what applications and data your desktop is going to be accessing and interacting with.

If you can, try and ensure that all your desktops, applications, user data and anything else are hosted in the same resource location for optimal user experience. Because that's one of the reasons why we do Citrix in the first place, right? (And yes, I know there are many more!) 😊

**"The time taken for a packet to be transferred across a network. You can measure this as one-way to its destination or as a round trip."**

– Latency

**"The factory of the future will have only two employees, a man, and a dog. The man will be there to feed the dog. The dog will be there to keep the man from touching the equipment."**

– Alice Kahn

# Hybrid and multi Cloud

***Submitted by:***

**Name:** Rory Monaghan **Country:** Ireland **Company:** Algiz Technology

www.linkedin.com/in/rory-monaghan

www.rorymon.com

@Rorymon

Much like in an on-premises datacenter, it is important to avoid vendor lock-in when working in the public Cloud. Most organizations venturing into the public Cloud today are leveraging hybrid Cloud and still consuming plenty of on-prem services and resources. Managing your VM templates and images across multiple Clouds and your on-prem datacenter can be challenging.

There is no "one size fits all" option. That is where Citrix App Layering can provide great value. It allows you to create a single image as an OS Layer and through its platform layers and various connectors, take that image and deploy it to any major hypervisor or Cloud with no learning curve. The tool applies the standards and logic for you!

***"While most CIOs have now identified the benefits Cloud can have on their business, worries over vendor lock-in can still be a major obstacle to adoption. Freedom of Information requests carried out this year found a third of UK local councils, for example, cite vendor lock-in as a barrier to adopting public Cloud services."*** – Ian Barker @BetaNews

***Submitted by:***

**Name:** Ned Bellavance **Country:** US. **Job role:** Founder
**Company:** Ned in the Cloud LLC

www.linkedin.com/in/ned-bellavance-ba68a52

www.nedinthecloud.com

@ned1313

When it comes to using the Cloud, especially in a hybrid-Cloud or multi-Cloud situation, consistency is absolutely key. Using ten different tools to manage ten different Clouds is the way to madness. Instead, pick a toolset that works across all of your environments and learn to wield that toolset expertly.

For each environment you should also be applying a consistent model when it comes to deployment, operations, security, monitoring, and cost management. Sometimes you will find yourself in a single-vendor Cloud, and thus you can avail yourself of the vendor native tooling. Other times you will be in a heterogeneous environment, and need to adopt third-party tools for management.

***"Regardless of the situation, first determine your technical requirements and then find tools that meet those requirements now and in the foreseeable future."*** – Ned Bellavance

***Submitted by:***

**Name:** Ivan de Mes **Country:** Netherlands **Job role:** Solution Architect EUC

www.linkedin.com/in/ivandemes

 www.ivandemes.com

 @ivandemes

If your business is fully dependent on the Cloud, consider a multi-Cloud strategy to reduce the risk of no or reduced availability whenever one Cloud provider has issues. Also focus on service level agreements that fit your company's requirements.

More than once I have seen companies going directly "all-in" into Cloud services and (partly) failing. Start small, test/experience required functionalities. Once successful, expand gradually.

When moving to the Cloud (services), think about who will manage it. Do you choose a managed services provider or your own IT personnel? For the latter, make sure IT personnel are able to manage the Cloud (services). Send IT personnel to training courses in advance before moving to production.

***"When consuming virtual machines from an IaaS provider, use automation or power plans to pause or shutdown virtual machines whenever they don't have to be used to reduce cost."*** – Ivan de Mes

Remember the guys picking up tapes and taking them to an off-site location? Still necessary? Public Cloud is perfect for backup and recovery and should be considered for both on-premises, public, and hybrid Clouds.

***Submitted by:***

**Name:** Alexander Tate **Country:** US. **Company:** CenturyLink

in www.linkedin.com/in/alex-tate-12b3387

As with all things, you should always have a *hybrid mindset*.
Lots of the industry is hard-locked into one or two technologies for Cloud/datacenter/software, etc. You should have the breadth of knowledge to take the approach and suggest the solution which meets the business requirements regardless of cost.
Read that again. You have to be the one to suggest that the company shells out some serious cash to get the results desired from a design.

You miss 100% of the shots you do not take. If you miss, no big deal: you shoot again until you hit one. The burden of getting financial approval only rests upon you to the point where you have shown that the best solution is X and not Y.

If Y is chosen, that's life, you move on and have already documented why Y was not the right choice. If the project bellyflops you know you did the right thing ethically. If you are right ethically and someone else isn't, you'll be much happier at the end of the day even if it means a change in scenery after the project is scrapped.

***Submitted by:***

**Name:** Andrei Vlad **Country:** Romania **Job role:** L3 Virtualization & OS Technical Specialist

in www.linkedin.com/in/vladandrei1987

I see more and more people concentrating on either private Clouds, or public Cloud services like Azure, AWS, GCP, and so on. Depending on the industry, I think its best people focus on what's best for them, and try to find the perfect balance between public and private Clouds. This balance will allow for things to be quickly and easily managed, while allowing for efficient recovery and data protection as well.

**"Doing off-premise is like shitting while away from home. Never feels as good as on premise."**

– Cláudio Rodrigues

***Submitted by:***

**Name:** Bob Molenaar **Country:** Netherlands **Job role:** Business Consultant **Company:** Salomon IT

www.linkedin.com/in/bob-molenaar-5629404

www.salomon-it.blog

During my daily visits to various customer sites throughout the week, I often get confronted with the question if, how, and why they (the customer) should move to the Cloud. A fair question, of course. Unfortunately there's no easy or straightforward answer.

Different customers have different use cases, and future plans. While the Cloud can help with most, it's no silver bullet. There simply are too many decencies. And I don't mean that in a bad way. I just feel that you have to go for whatever solution fits best, that's all.

What about *traditional* applications, for example? These will *haunt* us for many more years to come. Proper action needs to be taken, especially when the Cloud is taken into consideration. Than we have data. Is it stored on-premises, in the Cloud, or perhaps it's a combination of both?

Separating compute resources and data is usually not a good idea. But also, are there any specific company policies or regulations that need to be taken into consideration? The list basically goes on.

When assessing if Cloud fits, taking a step-by-step approach usually works best. Talk to the business (stakeholders), the users: find out what the functional and/or business requirements are. What are they satisfied with? In other words, what works, and what does not. Without a solid UX and happy users, your project will fail no matter how much money you spend, or what type of products/technologies you are planning on using – it's that simple.

Technology. What does the current environment and architecture look like? Eventually, all this should give you an idea of what is needed, from a technical as well as a business perspective.

As mentioned, Cloud technologies play a big part in all this, but there can be many reasons to also stay on-premises, or go *hybrid* with (big) parts of what you already have. The way we work and do business is getting more *Cloudy* by the day, yes, but one step at a time.

***Submitted by:***

**Name:** Rory Monaghan **Country:** Ireland **Company:** Algiz Technology

www.linkedin.com/in/rory-monaghan

www.rorymon.com

@Rorymon

Back in 2011, many major news outlets reported that the Cloud was going to wipe out thousands of IT jobs. It's 2019 and that hasn't happened yet. If anything, in this transition period with most organizations preferring hybrid Cloud, more jobs have been created because of it.

I have known IT pros who have felt threatened by the Cloud. I feel it is an opportunity to cast aside some of the mundane menial tasks and instead focus on innovation.

A quick win and gain for enterprise IT is that for each service you support that moves to an SaaS model, that's one less server or set of servers you need to patch. For every web-based SaaS app that's one less application we have to package and deploy.

The role of the IT pro is not becoming redundant, it is merely transforming.

***Submitted by:***

**Name:** Thomas Poppelgaard **Country:** Denmark **Job role:** Independent Consultant **Company:** Poppelgaard.com

www.linkedin.com/in/thomaspoppelgaard

www.poppelgaard.com

@_POPPELGAARD

Is public Cloud strategy only one thing to do, or is hybrid Cloud the best strategy? Hybrid Cloud will be here for a while before customers go all in public Cloud. Why it's all about the data, migrate legacy systems and coexists, the other thing is also having local assistance with a local Cloud provider team who helps customers to accelerate the Cloud journey.

You can have the best Cloud, but if you don't have any local presence customers don't get the human factor in digital transformation. It's very popular with customers around the world now moving servers to a local Cloud provider who takes care of this + provides access to public Clouds.

***Submitted by:***

**Name:** Rory Monaghan **Country:** Ireland **Company:** Algiz Technology

www.linkedin.com/in/rory-monaghan

www.rorymon.com

@Rorymon

The former COO of Google Cloud Platform, Diane Bryant spoke at the Citrix Synergy keynote in 2018 and stressed the importance of avoiding vendor lock-in when choosing Cloud products. That is a very smart approach: when building a physical datacenter today, you're not going to go all in on one vendor's products.

If you do that and want to or need to change in the future, it could be very challenging and expensive. The same rings true for the Cloud. Not only is this a sound approach to reduce the chance of a painful and costly transition in the future, but from a service redundancy standpoint this approach also makes sense.

If you have all of your eggs in one basket and there's a multi-hour outage, it's better if only some of your key services are affected rather than all of them!

With that in mind, as Azure, AWS, GCP and others continue to evolve, they each have products and services that appeal. For an enterprise deeply entrenched in Windows today who are just now looking at Cloud services, Microsoft Azure will be very appealing with Azure Active Directory, Office 365, Microsoft MFA and more in high demand. Azure Active Directory and Microsoft's MFA may make a lot of sense for your organization.

Whereas you may want to leverage AWS for high-end computing and for AWS AppStream or any of a number of its great tools, not to mention the fact that they partner with VMware who are already in so many enterprise datacenters today.

Google Cloud Platform could make a lot of sense for big data projects and use in areas that Google already lead the market in. Why not leverage each and play to their strengths

# Desktop as a Service & Office 365

***Submitted by:***

**Name:** Ruben Spruijt **Country:** Netherlands **Job role:** Sr. Technologist **Company:** Nutanix

www.linkedin.com/in/rspruijt

@rspruijt

*Note that these are two submissions merged into one.*

**Ruben's perspective on Cloud Services, Digital Workspaces, DaaS and duct tape.**

**Rockets are landing vertically**

5 years ago rockets were not landing vertically: the times are changing fast and fun times are ahead! Good enough user experience is no longer good enough.

The new workforce is coming in with higher expectations than ever before. And we need to design, provide and maintain modern digital workspaces with different products, services and processes to meet their needs. Also, we need to focus even more on delivering a great user experience, and use new Remote User Experience monitoring solutions to de-suckify a bad user experience.

A new era of innovative End-User Computing solutions is needed. These solutions and services will provide business consumers access to Windows applications and Desktop-as-a-Service are built and designed in the multi-Cloud era.

They combine the simplicity, best user, administrator and developer experience with the most powerful hybrid and public Cloud infrastructure technologies behind them. There are no old roads to new directions.

## Digital Workspace

Enterprise VDI and Desktop-as-a-Service (DaaS), which contain RemoteApps – RDSH, virtual desktops, persistent and non-persistent solutions, are a key element in today's digital workspace to support you and me to get stuff done. Some people, including great community friends, believe in the Year of VDI.

While I believe, I don't believe 'the Year of VDI' is happening today or in the future. Why? Because the biggest competitor isn't Amazon Workspace vs. Citrix XenDesktop vs. Nutanix Xi Frame vs. Microsoft WVD vs. VMware Horizon. No, it is the physical PC, the mobile device w/ apps, web – and Software as a Service.

Today's reality is – the digital workspace is a healthy mix of mobile apps, SaaS and Windows apps. This won't change anytime soon. For sure, different Windows applications will run native on a Windows PC while other applications will run on Remote Desktops or as RemoteApps.

We do spend more and more time in the browser, hence more and more customers do focus on applications and running them in a browser, and care less about a Windows Virtual Desktop. Wouldn't it be great to run any software in a browser? Think Windows Applications and Desktops are gone in 2025-2030? Think again!

## Duct Tape isn't born in the Cloud

With public Cloud you buy agility: focus on OPEX and that means growth for some and survival for others. Modern Desktop-as-a-Service solutions born in the public Cloud era means: multi-Cloud, multi-region, hybrid-Cloud, pay for use, Agile, OpEx-driven, flexible usage, fast time to market, highly innovative w/ updates happening weekly, high availability and agility, elastic by design.

The real attraction of public Cloud ought to be around making consumption simple. If public Cloud adoption is only being done to save money, it's a wrong driver to start with.

More competition between Amazon, Citrix, Microsoft, Nutanix, and VMware with regard to Desktop-as-a-Service is happening which is great –'rising tides lift all boats'.

***"Some of the established vendors try to (duct tape) transform their 'born in on-premises era' product and deliver this as a service in the public Cloud, while others design and build solutions with public Cloud services as the starting point."***
– Ruben Spruijt

The born-in-public Cloud services are disrupting the status quo.

This happened with services like Salesforce and Office 365, and is happening with DaaS. 'We live in a world where everybody is working together and at the same time everybody is competing'.

**The rise of Desktop-as-a-Service**

Desktop-as-a-Service designed and built in the public Cloud era means: API-driven, multi-tenant, multi-Cloud, hybrid-Cloud. Also, delightful and simple to use admin and user interfaces to launch applications (and desktops) as a service.

Does this mean all windows applications and desktops will run in the public Cloud? No, it means more variety of great options in the business toolbox to choose from.

My advice: choose wisely, understand business requirements, technology landscape and organizational readiness to change.

Also understand the 'data strategy' which includes a good practice that applications follow the data because business consumers get the best experience when applications and data are well connected.

This is one of the reasons why Desktop-as-a-Service is getting so much attention in multi-Clouds. Hybrid DaaS means the backplane is running as a service, operated by a service provider, and the actual workers – the VMs to run apps – can run in any available public Cloud region including your on-premises or hosted datacenter

**Outpost!**

Great solutions and developments are happening in the modern on-premises datacenter. Data locality, cost and cost control, and regulation are key reasons why many organizations build a modern datacenter.

Modern Hyper-Converged Infrastructure (HCI) solutions are able to simplify and create agility even when the customer owns the infrastructure and thereby keeps costs predictable and in check. Think building Hybrid Cloud is only for traditional IT vendors?

Please, think again … why do Microsoft and Amazon build solutions like 'Azure Stack' and 'Outpost'? Because they and others like Nutanix see a great future and reality in multi-Clouds including Hybrid. Hybrid Cloud is about and breaking down the infrastructure silos, API-friendly infrastructure that makes automation possible. Disrupting and improving the way enterprises think about and manage their public and private Cloud computing is the task of vendors, consultants, partners – awesome!

***Submitted by**:*

**Name:** Scott Manchester **Country:** US. **Job role:** Group Manager RDS/WVD **Company:** Microsoft

www.linkedin.com/in/smanchester

www.microsoft.com

@RDS4U

Windows Virtual Desktop is a new Azure service to manage virtualization environments – it is a differentiated offering, providing a significantly better user and ITPro experience as compared to other public Cloud virtualization offerings. WVD provides a significant advantage over the competitors as it enables a multi-user Windows 10 experience, combines both application and desktop remoting, and includes rights to run Windows 7 with Extended Security Updates for free (customer pays for IaaS)!

To contextualize this, a quick summary of how enterprises use desktop + app virtualization today will help. Today we have approximately 100m active users of virtualization – where they access Windows Applications and Desktops for an enterprise-hosted virtualization environment. About 95% of Microsoft's top 500 customers use some form of desktop or application virtualization.

On any given day over 2 million of our enterprise users run Office applications using virtualization – traditionally this has been a challenge in non-persistent environments, where limitations include suboptimal performance in Outlook in cache mode, no support for OneDrive, and overall UX limitations. With Windows Virtual Desktop we are delivering an Office experience that addresses the key gaps in remoting O365, delivering an experience that is on a par with Office on a local device.

WVD began as an investigation to the growth of "Desktop as a Service" aka "DaaS" and, if there was a business opportunity, to capture that potentially growing business on Azure. Gartner and IDC predict explosive growth in this space with over 30% YoY growth and a target of over $3b in revenue by 2019.

With a charter from the SLT to create a differentiated offering in this space, we pivoted our Remote Desktop Modern Infrastructure (RDmi) App services to a first party-hosted service and platform. The reception to the initial idea, a recent quote from one of the foremost analysts in this space – *"Customers are demanding more flexibility and an offering that prioritizes security as well as management. I think you are ticking all of those boxes."*

Windows Virtual Desktop is an example of opportunity meets execution. The RDS team had developed a similar offering called Azure RemoteApp about 3 years earlier.

This product was not well received by customers and had significant overhead to maintain. The product was ultimately deprecated and the RDS team went back to the drawing board based on the learning from that experience.

***"We became much more data-driven – gathering insight from one-on-one meetings with customers and partners and targeted questionnaires to our vast customer base using virtualization today."***
– Scott Manchester

We purchased all of the analyst reports and digested all their insights and predictions. We worked with the business development team to gather insights into competing in-market products, and from all this data we shaped the features and capabilities of Windows Virtual Desktop.

The decision to shut down Azure RemoteApp was very difficult as the product took years to develop and had only been available in market for around 18 months.

It turned out to be one of the key elements to enable us to step back and develop a new product without the overhead of managing a live service. It was a classic example of "*The Innovators Dilemma*", a topic introduced in a book by Clayton M. Christensen Get it here:

https://www.amazon.com/Innovators-Dilemma-Technologies-ManagementInnovation/dp/1633691780/ref=sr_1_1?ie=UTF8&qid=1541002111&sr=8-1&keywords=the+innovators+dilemma

The book discussed the challenges of innovating while supporting in-market products.

***Submitted by:***

**Name:** Thomas Poppelgaard **Country:** Denmark **Job role:** Independent Consultant **Company:** Poppelgaard.com

www.linkedin.com/in/thomaspoppelgaard

www.poppelgaard.com

@_POPPELGAARD

WVD will help customers digitally transform their existing on-prem physical workstation or traditional on prem VDI/RDS. Microsoft have the best platform now in Azure with WVD, as it allows virtualization of Windows 7 desktops with Extended Security Updates, which enables support of Windows 7 until January 2023. This gives users a comprehensive solution for Windows 7 desktops and apps alongside those for Windows 10 and Windows Server. It's all about supporting legacy systems in the digital transformation to WVD, and Microsoft provides that.

***Submitted by:***

**Name:** David Wilkinson **Country:** Great Britain **Job role:** EUC Architect **Company:** WilkyIT

www.linkedin.com/in/david-wilkinson-90113311

www.wilkyit.com

@WilkyIT

Deploying Office 365 is a journey most of us have started, finished or are soon embarking upon. Here are some tips/hints I would recommend:

- Moving to Office 365 will not negate the need for storage locally (I know some will be shocked by this), you'll still need storage on local devices for caching data (i.e. OneDrive, Outlook OST).
- 1TB Mailbox/OneDrive Maximum is the default allocation on Office 365. An educated guess on storage required locally should be taken based on averages on the existing document & mailbox of users. This is a major adjustment from controlled managed mailbox/My Documents!
- End-User Experience is King! Caching your Office 365 delivers the best performance.
- RDSH/Shared Devices/Kiosks PC (which are common in healthcare) will accumulate multiple caches for each user and sufficient storage need to be allocated or alternative solution to redirect storage to alternative location.
- RDSH-based solutions (i.e Citrix, VMware Horizon) which are non-persistent need to redirect the caches off the local server, otherwise a poor experience will be felt re-creating everyone's login.
- Third-party tools are available for redirecting your local caching needs from a physical desktop (FSLogix, Liquidware, Ivanti Workspace Manager) or RDSH (Citrix UPM, VMware App Volumes or Microsoft UPD)

- Do not inspect/scan traffic bound for Office 365 and, if possible, bypass proxy as per MS recommendation. Microsoft ExpressRoute will NOT in most cases be granted solely for Office 365 only.
- Please enable MFA! Username & password are no longer considered secure enough!

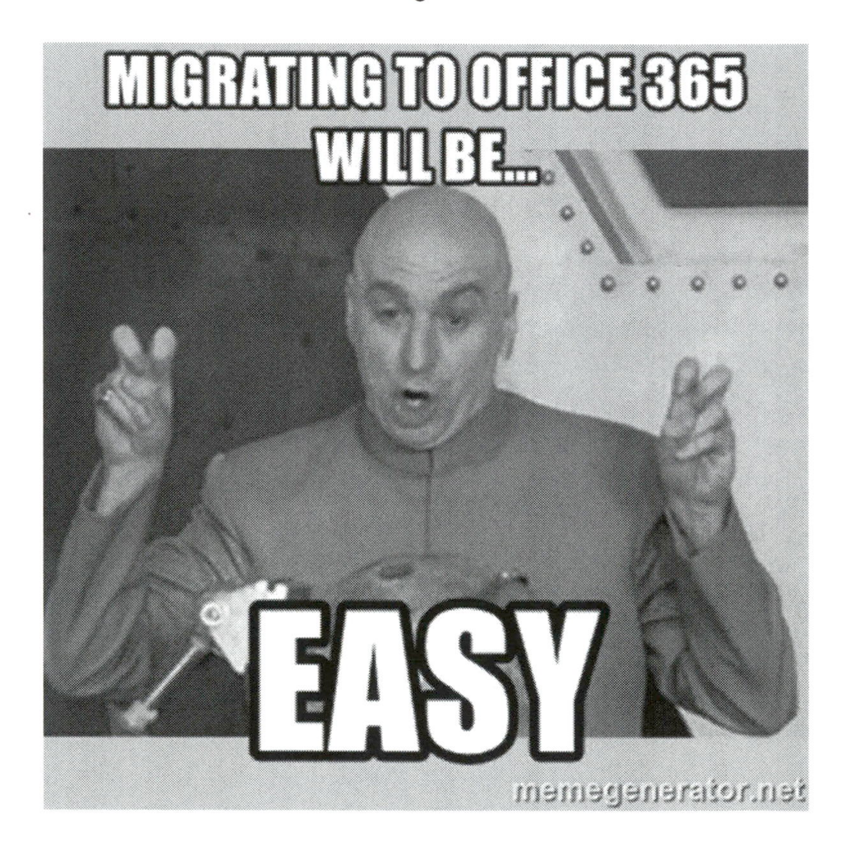


***"Moving to Office 365 will not negate the need for storage locally (I know some will be shocked by this), you'll still need storage on local devices for caching data (i.e. OneDrive, Outlook OST)."***
– David Wilkinson

***Submitted by:***

**Name:** Stefan Georgiev **Country:** US. **Job role:** Product Manager RDS/WVD **Company:** Microsoft

www.microsoft.com

*Note that these are two submissions merged into one.*

## Thoughts on Azure Storage, user profiles and Windows Virtual Desktop / Remote Desktop Service

In this document we will review user profiles, interactions with Azure Storage and how those work in Windows Virtual Desktop, and to a lesser extend RDS 2016 in Azure. For those not familiar with Windows Virtual Desktop it was announced on 3/21 https://www.microsoft.com/microsoft-365/partners/news/article/announcing-windows-virtual-desktop

In addition, we will go over user profile disks and their future, how Azure Storage is currently used in VDI / RDSH environments, where there are the opportunities to improve storage performance and cost. We review some common best practices. Finally, we will look at some interesting options that are possible with Windows Virtual Desktop, FSLogix and Azure Files.

## User Profiles / User Profile Disk (UPD)

User profiles introduce a layer of abstraction that allow us to remove user data and settings from the operating system. User profiles are common for VDI and RDSH environments where users are not guaranteed that they will be using the same VM upon returning to establish a new session. We can call these types of environments non-persistent.

By storing user data and user settings in a separate layer it allows for users to feel like they are returning to the same VM day after day, despite this not being true. It is even possible that the original VM does not exist anymore but has been replaced.

Historically Microsoft has attempted quite a few takes on profile solutions with different degrees of success; a few that come to mind are roaming user profile enterprise state roaming, and user profile disks (UPD). In RDS 2016 on Azure, UPDs were the Microsoft-approved option.

**FSLogix profile containers and user profile disk (UPD)**

Before moving forward, it needs to be called out that our discussion will focus on FSLogix profile containers (FSLogix office containers being a subset of FSLogix profile containers) and to a large extent ignore UPD. The main reason for ignoring UPD is that with the acquisition of FSLogix, Microsoft is moving away for UPD and embracing FSLogix profile containers.

There are quite a few reasons why. However, the one that is most applicable in a VDI / RDSH environment is the fact that FSLogix profile containers are capable of abstracting user data and settings away from the VMs.

This is important as changes and update of the VM and its operating system will not impact the user data stored in the profile. Additionally, the performance benefits of FSLogix help keep main login times low and reads/writes over the network comparatively low.

**VDI, VMs and disks in Azure**

When a VM is provisioned in Azure there are three main components tied to it: storage, compute and network.

Here we will focus on storage. Disks in Azure are VHDs that live on Azure Page Blob. There is an operating system disk (C:\) and a temporary disk (D:\). While the operating system disk is indeed a VHD file, the D:\ drive is a physical drive.

Azure's best practices recommend that no relevant data is stored on the temporary disk. This D:\ drive is used for things like page files and some other intensive read/write operations.

In VDI environments a common practice is to add an additional drive, set up for user data (E:\). This is done to persist user data and allows enterprise administrations to rebuild the VMs without having to worry about user data.

There are many ways to allocate user data to the E:\ drive. Common folders (My Documents, etc.) can be pointed to this drive via the operating system; some applications allow their data to be moved to a different drive (like Outlook). There are challenges with this approach. User data on the E:\ drive is not stateless, meaning that if moved to another VM certain operations and data may need to be performed again.

There is administrative and cost overhead associated with this extra disk. Further security is also challenging as the VHD tied with the E:\ disk can be attached to the wrong VM or, worse, a malicious attacker can obtain access to it. Additionally, if the enterprise already has OneDrive for business to store user data, they now need to pay for yet another copy of the data.

If we look in RDSH environments it's common for user data to live on a network share. This scenario is like what we have been doing on-premises. However, a network share is tied with additional cost and administrative burden. This network share needs to be performant in order not to bottleneck users' login times. The "how performant?" question has a "depends" answer.

It depends on how many users are to be served by the environment and what are the requirements of the profiling solution.

With UPD, Microsoft encourage using S2D SOFS cluster as storage infrastructure when it comes to RDS 2016 in Azure. There is a great article here: https://docs.microsoft.com/en-us/windows-server/remote/remote-desktop-services/rds-storage-spaces-direct-deployment) that covers a lot of the details around S2D SOFS. Over time few challenges have arisen.

Setting up an S2D SOFS looks deceptively easy. However, there are many traps along the way. For example, when building a cross-region S2D SOFS there is usually at least one firewall in the way. That firewall may not be able to keep up with the amount of transactions and bring S2D SOFS replication down.

Further S2D SOFS are expensive to run in Azure even if Cloud witness is being used, which is what Microsoft recommends. Maintenance of the cluster nodes themselves is an involved process as the operating system needs to be updated and kept secure.

**Alternative S2D SOFS**

Azure Files is an alternative for S2D SOFS. It takes away the issues with cost and administrative overhead. Azure Files, however, is not the perfect solution.

There is limited support for Azure AD integration. There is a preview of a feature that allows Azure File share to be authenticated via Azure Active Directory Domain Services (Azure AD DS). Additionally, to match the performance of S2D SOFS are required and that feature is also in preview.

Once those features are GA an environment can be built where user profiles are stored on Azure Files. An even better option is in the future, as last year (2018) at Ignite the Azure Files team mentioned the possibility of integrating Azure Files with an on-premises domain controller. This will be the linchpin as enterprises are reluctant to use Azure AD DS due to its limited feature set.

**Bright future**

One interesting convergence point of FSLogix profile containers, Windows Virtual Desktop and Azure Files is the possibility to use Azure Files to store the profile container, by utilizing FSLogix redirection of reads and writes from the operating system disk (C:\) to an Azure Files share.

The Azure File share is authenticated via an on-premises domain controller, hence is using the identity of the user. These will allow us to reduce the operating system disk size to fit operating system and applications. All user data will be living in Azure Files.

***"By using some conservative calculations in Azure calculator, the total cost of storage can drop anywhere between 20% and 40%, based on Azure Files consumption and original size of the system disk. Azure Files brings a list of benefits to the table."*** – Stefan Georgiev

Back-ups become automated even with locally redundant storage. No need for enterprise administrators to set up backup automation. Azure File Sync can be used for burst to Azure type of scenarios where user profiles from an RDS 2016 on-premises solution are replicated in Azure to handle loads via either Windows Virtual Desktop or RDS 2016 on Azure.

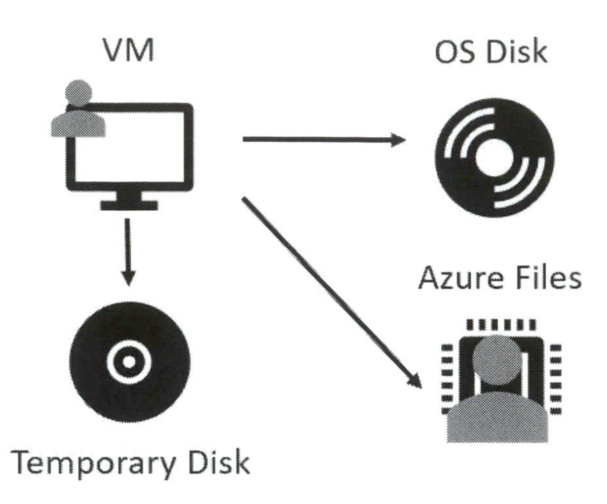


**User state back-ups**

Often when it comes to back up in RDSH / VDI environments enterprise administrators follow a process that has been established for physical machines: more precisely, the entire VM gets backed up. The backup includes operating system, applications, and user data.

When running Windows Virtual Desktop or RDS 2016 on Azure, best practice recommendation is to use a master image that already has the operating system and applications configured. If this is combined with FSLogix profile container (even for a VDI-persistent environment) it allows us to back up the user data and settings only (the FSLogix profile container).

When we need to rebuild or rollback we spin up a new VM that already has operating system and applications and just introduce the FSLogix profile container. This will not always be applicable. In some highly regulated verticals, back-ups and snapshots must include the VM state (logs, setting, etc.): when this is required the entire VM needs to be backed up / snapshotted.

***Submitted by***:

**Name:** Niels Kok **Country:** Netherlands **Company:** Avensus **Job role:** Technical Specialist

www.linkedin.com/in/niels-kok-79823360

www.avansus.nl

Securing Exchange Online (Office 365)

Securing Exchange Online and its data became a hot topic last year because of Europe's new GDPR requirements. One way to secure your clients and their data is to block basic authentication and use modern authentication for all Exchange Online services. In this scenario I assume that your client has the licenses needed to use the client software mentioned below.

Blocking basic authentication means that you need to use the newest Microsoft Office clients to authenticate to Exchange Online. So, you need to use:

- Outlook mobile for Android and iOS
- Outlook 2016 for Windows machines
- Outlook for Mac 2016 for Macintosh

You can't use the native Apps on Android and iOS anymore to configure your corporate email. This also means that the native Macintosh Mail application which Mac users like to use is not configurable for corporate email. You also can't use the native Mail app on Windows anymore.

Combine this with the App Protection policies in Intune and you can secure your data even more. For example, for you can block "taking a screenshot" or "copying text" from the Outlook Mobile App.
Users can configure their corporate email on their private phones but they need to do so in Outlook Mobile which you protect with the app protection policy in Intune.

***Submitted by:***

**Name:** Kevin Goodman **Country:** US. **Job role:** Industry Gadfly
**Company:** TBD

With the recent Microsoft announcements, here are some alternatives to Office 365 on Windows Server 2019.

Windows Server 2019, which shipped late in 2018, provides no support for Office 365. Besides, support for Office 365 on Server 2016 ends in 2025. If you support your Office 365 ProPlus users on Server 2016 RD Session Host, you need to prepare for this situation.

Here are some alternatives:

**Office 2019 Perpetual**

Office 2019 is Microsoft's latest standalone Office productivity suite. It is a subset of the applications available in Office 365. The features that are missing are the collaboration pieces (the ability to share documents online or use Cloud storage with OneDrive). As opposed to paying monthly, Microsoft sells Office 2019 perpetual as a one-time purchase.

You pay a single, upfront cost to get Office apps for one device. It is essential to understand that the device is the machine that you access RDSH with, not the server itself. Each user must have a license, even though you install Office 2019 once on the server.

**Endpoint considerations**

Depending upon which endpoint you have, you may be able to avoid needing Office 365 on Server 2019 by installing it on the endpoint.

For example, if your users have Windows endpoints or suitable mobile endpoints, such as iOS devices, then one solution is to install Office 365 directly on the endpoint and run a hybrid solution.

### Competing Office Software: LibreOffice or G Suite

Not all office suite software comes from Microsoft. Many consider third-party solutions such as the open-source, LibreOffice, or Google's G Suite to be valid alternatives. These suites offer the collaboration features that many of your users need at a significantly lower cost.

### WVD

Lastly, another alternative to running Office 365 on Server 2019 is to migrate to Windows Virtual Desktops and utilize one of their partners such as CloudJumper or Workspot. In this scenario, Microsoft permits Office 365 installations on virtual machines running either Windows 10 or Windows Multi-user.

An important point to note: this Cloud-based alternative may not work for you, depending upon your requirements. It is Azure-only and results in Cloud lock-in, but it is currently the solution that Microsoft is driving.

**"To all users of technology who are willing to take a chance, make a choice, and try a new way of doing things so that we can nurture and enjoy a happy, healthy planet."**

– Katherine Murray

# Security & Identity

***Submitted by:***

**Name:** Patrick Coble **Country:** US. **Job role:** Security Architect
**Company:** VDISEC

www.linkedin.com/in/vdihacker

www.vdisecurity.org

@VDIHacker

**Self-Signed Certificates**

When deploying many solutions, they use self-signed SSL certificates and you should replace them as soon as you can. Think about that application you work on that you are in every day that you just accept the certificate warning and then usually enter your username and password to do your work.

There is a risk that if an attacker is in your deployment, they could be a Man in the Middle, and you just accepted their certificate because that is what you do every day to work on that system.

You should replace this with a domain-issued certificate that your computer will trust or if you are the only person who uses the system then trust that certificate and never administer the system from another one which in most cases may be very impractical. If you do not have a PKI deployment it could be worth deploying: there are many step-by-step guides out there.

***Submitted by:***

**Name:** René Bigler **Country:** Switzerland

www.linkedin.com/in/rené-bigler-3394b4130

www.dreadysblog.com

@dready73

Probably one of your first steps towards the Cloud is looking to replace some of your existing on-premises applications and services with SaaS apps.

One of the first workloads coming to your mind might be Microsoft Office and its corresponding server products such as Microsoft Exchange and SharePoint Server. Those are great candidates to start your journey to the Cloud.

But as soon as you are looking at other non-Microsoft Cloud services it's important to have a closer look at how those SaaS solutions handle the user provisioning and authentication. One thing you definitely want to avoid is creating separate user entities for every single service you're going to implement.

Think about the time and effort you as an administrator would waste by managing all those user entities in all the different Cloud services. But also, from an end-user experience standpoint it would be a nightmare if they had to remember different usernames and passwords for every single Cloud service.

To avoid all this hassle, it's important to define an identity provider (IdP) at an early stage of your Cloud journey and federate the authentication procedures from your Cloud services to this single identity provider whenever possible.

Possible candidates for acting as such an identity provider might be Microsoft Azure AD, Google Apps for Business, Okta, etc. These services usually allow you to act as identity service for other parties (your SaaS apps) by providing authentication, authorization and in some cases even user provisioning through industry-standard protocols such as OAuth 2.0, OpenID Connect and SAML.

**Are you planning to move some of your on-premises workloads to the Cloud?**

That's great but be aware that a lift-and-shift approach is not always the best way to go.

***"Whenever possible try to leverage purpose-built Cloud services for your use case."*** – René Bigler

Usually those provide a better performance, higher availability and are cheaper than running your own virtual machine with your service on top in the Cloud.

As an example, you could use Azure Active Directory or Azure Active Directory Domain Services to synchronize on-premises directories and enable single sign-on or join Azure virtual machines to a domain without domain controllers. If it suits your needs, this is the easier and cheaper option than building and running your own domain controller virtual machine in Azure.

**Sponsored content**

**ControlUp Real-Time Console**
Easily monitor and manage through the console's actionable dashboard and quickly resolve issues on hypervisors, virtual and physical servers, user sessions, application processes, and more.

**Real-Time view drilldown**
See your entire infrastructure in a simple, logical, and elegant spreadsheet-like view. Each cell is updated every 3 seconds and the view is easily searchable and sortable by columns, allowing you to quickly spot stressed resources, and drill down and investigate them in depth with a click of a button.

**Triggers and Alerts**
ControlUp's set-and-forget takes the worry out of monitoring. Simply click your way through alert creation options, and be notified in any way you want, from setting an audio chime, to email alerts, push notifications, and sending the relevant event info to another system.

**ControlUp Insights**
Focus on what you need to know to make sure your IT infrastructure is at its best. Our big data analytics platform identifies trends and provides truly actionable findings.

It also helps you optimize resource allocations among monitored servers and desktops. It provides recommendations for optimizing the CPU and RAM allocations of each computer.

Get in touch with us here: https://www.controlup.com/contact-us

***Submitted by:***

**Name:** Jason Samuel **Country:** US. **Job role:** Solutions Architect and Security Practice Lead **Company:** Alchemy Tech Group

www.linkedin.com/in/jasonsamuel

www.jasonsamuel.com

@_JasonSamuel

For anything end-user facing related to the Cloud, identity and access management is the key to being successful. When you move a workload to your Cloud tenant or migrate to an SaaS web app in someone's Cloud, you have to carefully consider how the users will get to "their stuff".

This is what makes them productive. If it's not a uniform and user-friendly experience, it breaks the user's momentum and over time these compound and have a great detriment to productivity. If you leave this area very lax and depend on the Cloud vendor for security, you can quickly lose control and visibility as to what is coming into and out of this new Cloud-based perimeter.

Moving anything to the Cloud does not mean security is the Cloud vendor's responsibility now: it is still very much on you. I always suggest a few things to consider in your design and approach it with two things in mind: end-user experience and security:

1. A single identity provider (IdP) in the Cloud that can sync from your on-prem directory to create a new "hybrid identity".
2. Use this modern authentication-capable IdP for single sign-on to all Cloud and SaaS delivery. A user should have only one company identity and therefore one password to access everything that belongs to the company.
3. Consider modern password-less options for your users in the interests of security and a better end-user experience.

4. Consider contextual access to "their stuff" that can be verified at the initial session login and continuously throughout the session. Example: Login via internal Wi-Fi on a company laptop gives full access to a sensitive app but then jumping to the coffee shop's external Wi-Fi across the street during a lunch break would be a context change and therefore limit access to some sensitive things until you are internal again.
5. Examine Cloud Access Security Brokers (CASBs) and data loss prevention (DLP) solutions to protect "their stuff" from leaving the controls of corporate IT, as well as to give visibility and tracking.
6. "Their stuff" is more important than the device and network they may be on. Work to protect the company's intellectual property and mitigate risk outward from it. Establishing device requirements and network requirements for access is good for extremely sensitive material, but can be an obstruction to productivity and mobility needs of a company when overreaching to all company material. Work to establish a strategy to classify material and determine sensible access requirement policies.

***"While the managed security services market at large is expected to grow to more than $40 billion by 2022, MSPs need to stay on top of their game in their respective markets to keep clients and remain competitive. A huge part of any MSPs product stack is their identity provider (IdP), which is the foundation."*** – George Lattimore @securityblvd

***Submitted by:***

**Name:** Patrick Coble **Country:** US. **Job role:** Security Architect
**Company:** VDISEC

www.linkedin.com/in/vdihacker

www.vdisecurity.org

@VDIHacker

**Byte-Size Security Nugget – MFA**

Passwords alone are not good enough for access to sensitive data and most likely your VDI deployment. Most VDI deployments are hosting their most critical business applications, so their security should be paramount. There are three major problems that have made this a much bigger problem than it was just 5-10 years ago.

There have been over 6.7 billion username and passwords leaked over the past 10 years. Password reuse, with 6.7 billion usernames and passwords around, is getting attacked daily, and the probability of successful attacks with old passwords is higher than you would think.

Using the same password for multiple sites means that when one is breached all are breached and when your users use the same or similar password for their personal accounts it is a threat to your corporate deployment.

Every major VDI solution has a way to support a multifactor authentication solution where someone will need the username, password and a device or access to a device. I do not recommend SMS-based solutions because of the spoofing and cloning that is possible. I recommend push applications and hardware tokens where possible.

In some deployments having MFA for all internal and external users may not be possible because of the workflow changes, but external is a must. If you MFA just external access don't forget any other service bound to AD from other services that don't require MFA so you don't have a blind side where someone can circumvent MFA.

**Promotion Layers**

Before making any production, changes and/or starting with lockdown initiative with policies, you want to ensure you have a multilayered promotion process before we start testing with our test server\desktop. We should never want to test changes in production.

I have been very successful using a 3-layer promotion process in some very large deployments. There may be a need for a couple of production layers in very large deployments to help mitigate risks of outages and slow the introduction of changes. The normal 3 layers I have used are test, staging\pre-production, and production. These layers allow application installs, configuration changes and Windows updates to be applied in a way to reduce the risk of impact to your users.

***"A good rule of IT is the more canaries (layers) in the coal mine, the better it will be for you and your users. If you can detect problems with a small percentage of users vs. all the users being impacted, that is a good day."*** – Patrick Coble

Some test deployments may have separate networks, domains and VDI sites, but the same process can still apply. Below are some of the normal layers I have seen along with some of the basic tests to do while at each layer. If you are able to test in the user context, that is the best way possible to make sure it works for them and not just admins.

- Test
  - This is the VM\Image that the changes are first deployed to.
  - Before Promoting to Staging basic smoke testing should be completed.
    - Does the device register?
    - Can you launch the application\desktop? (Test User Context)
    - Can you open the application in question? (Test User Context)
    - Does Printing or Peripheral Support work? (Test User Context)
  - In some deployments UAT may start here with real users; in others it is promoted to staging before UAT begins.

- Staging (Pre-Production)
  - UAT Testing is Conducted (Real\Power Users)
    - Can you launch the application\desktop?
    - Can you open the application in question?
    - Does Printing or Peripheral Support work?
    - Once Validated and Signed off the vDisk can be Promoted to Production.
    - This is when Change Control tickets should be entered, and the change should be scheduled.

- Production
  - In some cases, there may be multiple groups of Pools\Delivery Groups to promote to in succession to mitigate risk which will reduce the impact if there are issues found. I have seen 2-3 production layers most common in very large shops because that way only 33-50% of the users are impacted.
  - There will be some applications that you have to upgrade and go “All In” because you cannot

connect to them with the old version once it has been upgraded on the backend and/or frontend, or vice versa.

- Propagating the promotion can be done automatically with the scripts, imaging wizards or regular reboots. You may schedule your reboots nightly or weekly which will roll the update out if you are using something like Provisioning Services. Then if you are using a clone-based solution it will be scheduled within the wizard per Pool\Delivery Group to roll out the changes.

**"If you have built castles in the air, your work need not be lost; that is where they should be. Now put the foundations under them."** – Henry David Thoreau

***Submitted by:***

**Name:** Jack Madden **Country:** US. **Job role:** Blogger & Executive Editor **Company:** BrianMadden.com

www.linkedin.com/in/maddenjack

www.brianmadden.com

@JackMadden

It's time to learn about identity

Today, every end-user computing professional should be learning about identity management concepts, including single sign-on, authentication, conditional access, and zero trust.

We all have our specialties – perhaps VDI, mobility, or Windows – and, of course, we won't be abandoning these. But EUC is broader than any one of these areas, and identity is a topic that spans all of them.

There are many practical benefits to learning about identity.

Firstly, learning about authentication is a great way to get more confident with security topics. (It was only after I did this that I felt I could hold my own in deep security debates.) And multi-factor authentication is clearly one of the first tools we should adopt to help prevent data breaches.

With the growth of Cloud/web/SaaS apps, knowing about federation, and things like IdPs and SPs, SAML and OAuth, and provisioning workflows is essential. Cloud apps touch all of our endpoints, whether physical, virtual, or mobile, so we'll all have to deal with them at some point.

And remember back in the days when we talked about the consumerization of IT, Shadow IT, and FUIT? It turns out that many of the issues we worried about are now solved. More often than not, the answer is identity and access management.

Or, how about the vision of delivering any app to any user on any device in any location, another idea that we've been talking about for years. Again, the common layer that makes this work is identity, with a healthy dose of conditional access, zero trust, and analytics to help build policies and put everything together.

I now believe that identity, conditional access, and zero trust are the most important EUC trends since mobility and the Cloud, and that every EUC pro should get an introduction to identity.

***Submitted by:***

**Name:** Martin Zugec **Country:** US. **Job role:** Sr. Architect
**Company:** Citrix

www.linkedin.com/in/martinzugec

www.techzone.citrix.com

@MartinZugec

Companies that are moving towards the Cloud should be prepared to face many security challenges as well. Contrary to traditional, on-premises computing, it is often much easier to start new projects in the Cloud without involvement (and experience) of IT departments. Very often, different business units will use Cloud computing without central oversight and security controls.

There are many ways how this can be exploited by malicious actors. You are most probably going to be a target (if not a victim) of cryptojacking. The goal of this attack is simply to hijack virtualized resources (or Cloud account) and use it for the mining of cryptocurrencies.

Unlimited scaling of Cloud is obviously a very lucrative target for these attacks and it doesn't really matter if you are a small or large company, as long as your credit card is linked to the profile. Many companies suffer multiple cryptojacking attacks without even realizing it, as often business units will pay for the damages and not report it as a security incident.

There are two attacks to be aware of – hijacking your existing VMs, and running a cryptojacking workload on them (you'll probably first notice much higher utilization and slower response times from hijacked machines) and full-scale attacks where attackers will hijack your account and start spawning as many new powerful virtual machines as possible.

To prevent cryptojacking attacks, make sure that your Cloud instances are as secure as your on-premises ones, and follow all the security best practices – strong passwords, multi-factor authentication, monitor utilization of servers (and processes) and keep an eye on all security news.

Cryptojacking attacks and Cloud computing are a great match for each other and attackers behave differently – there is usually no immediate indicator of compromise (like with ransomware), as they try to stay hidden and leech your resources for as long as possible.

**"To prevent cryptojacking attacks, make sure that your Cloud instances are as secure as your on-premises ones, and follow all the security best practices – strong passwords, multi-factor authentication, monitor utilization of servers (and processes) and keep an eye on all security news."**

– Martin Zugec

***Submitted by:***

**Name:** Bill Sempf **Country:** US. **Job role:** Application Security Architect **Company:** Products Of Innovative New Technology

www.linkedin.com/in/billsempf

 www.sempf.net

 @sempf

They tell us the Cloud is more secure, and they are mostly right. We don't need to patch servers or worry about physical security when applications are hosted in the Cloud. However, the application running in the Cloud is just as insecure as ever, and the developer needs to take the same considerations into account as always.

In requirements gathering, they must consider those non-functional security requirements that get ignored by the business, like Encoding, Input Validation, Session Management, and CSRF Protection. The OWASP ASVS will go a long way to making sure the requirements for the application cover the full range of software security requirements.

When self-hosting, it is possible to arrange for internal support, but when a company Cloud-hosts, it is dependent on its Service Level Agreement with its Cloud provider. Developers should know how that SLA works. What happens in case of a breach? Is Denial of Service protection provided? Is there some common authentication system available? Make sure developers understand what the Cloud provider will do for the application before they code it into the application.

Data protection is more important in the Cloud than it is when self-hosting. Of course data should always be protected in transit with HTTPS. When Cloud-hosting an application, sensitive data must also be protected at rest with secure encryption.

The application is one misconfiguration away from spilling all of its data online, most of the time. Developers should know that encoding is not the same as encryption, and that a well-vetted, secure encryption library must be used.

When Cloud-hosting, the application is sharing a server with several other tenants. Strong fences make for good neighbors. Isolation, auditable administrative access, encryption, and change management are even more important when you don't know who your neighbors are.

Then there is data loss: not the hacker-stole-it kind, but something getting accidentally deleted. Having adequate off-site back-ups can prevent organizations from irreparable damage caused by data loss threats. Be ready for an incident. Model the potential for loss (or a security event), have a team ready with a plan, and be ready to act.

There are tools out there, in the public domain, for auditing a Cloud deployment. Azurite for Microsoft Azure and, and Duo's CloudMapper are great examples. Know what's out there, and protect it. Cloud-driven applications can bring a high level of security, but it is important to know how they can be similar and different from what development teams are used to.

***Submitted by:***

**Name:** Chaitanya **Country:** India

 @TechAssimilator

- Security Security Security... always revisit your Cloud security settings to make sure your data isn't public.
- Getting a Cloud service is similar to buying groceries from a store. You have everything available there. Just pay and use.

***Submitted by:***

**Name:** Aaron Parker **Country:** Australia **Job role:** Solution Architect **Company:** Insentra

www.linkedin.com/in/aaronedwardparker

www.stealthpuppy.com

@stealthpuppy

Disable Windows Hello for Business by default. Windows Hello for Business is a great feature of Windows 10 that you should be seeking to adopt to improve security (especially with secondary authentication mechanisms such as Universal 2nd Factor keys, Azure AD password-less sign-in, etc.), but if you're just adopting Windows 10 (either joined to an on-premises Active Directory domain or Azure AD-joined), Windows Hello can trip you up.

For example, a Windows Hello authentication is a local authentication and users won't obtain Kerberos keys making access services such as file shares difficult.

Disable Windows Hello for Business by default and pilot Windows Hello as you go. Windows Hello can be controlled via Group Policy or MDM policies and targeted to a pilot group to ensure that you have dependencies in place and integration with on-premises components including Active Directory Certificate Services working before it is rolled out across your entire environment.

***Submitted by:***

**Name:** Marius Sandbu **Country:** Norway **Job role:** Cloud Architect **Company:** EVRY

www.msandbu.org

 @msandbu

Moving to SaaS-based services will require a new way of thinking about security, with the shift away from perimeter-based security to identity-based security using the zero-trust model.

Many have already started to implement features such as Azure Active Directory Conditional Access together with risk control and MFA, but that only provides security on the authentication level and not any extra security on what kind of activities the end-users are doing.

With this adoption of SaaS, it is also important as part of your security & governance model to look at adding a CASB (Cloud Access Security Broker) product to it.

***"CASB provides security on SaaS on an API level and which allows it to be able to look at end-user activity and determine if certain activities are abnormal or not."*** – Marius Sandbu

Many CASB providers today have built-in API integrations with most of the commonly used SaaS services such as Office 365, Google G Suite, Salesforce and so on. However it is important to understand that a CASB solution is only as good as the APIs that it can use against the SaaS providers.

**"Unlike a drop of water which loses its identity when it joins the ocean, man does not lose his being in the society in which he lives. Man's life is independent. He is born not for the development of the society alone, but for the development of his self."** – B. R. Ambedkar

# Automation

***Submitted by:***

**Name:** Steve Noel **Country:** US. **Job role:** Citrix Consultant

www.linkedin.com/in/snoel

www.verticalagetechnologies.com

@Steve_Noel

PowerShell is just as important for Cloud implementations, just as much as on-premises implementations. They all have their own Tools/Modules to install. This will be a key part for automation, reporting, and all the benefits PowerShell brings.

AWS Specific: Note when using 'Get-EC2Instance' PowerShell command in AWS. **Get-EC2Instance** groups results by ReservationID, which can contain multiple items per line entry. Think of this like a receipt at a grocery store that could contain multiple items per receipt.

When using actions against this command, you could be affecting multiple instances, not just one. To focus on single instances only, use (**Get-EC2Instance**).Instances.

***Submitted by:***

**Name:** Chris Twiest **Country:** Netherlands **Job role:** Principal Consultant **Company:** Detron

www.linkedin.com/in/chris-twiest-a2378186

www.workspace-guru.com

@TwiestChris

In the era of Cloud computing, it's now become essential to know how to automate and use PowerShell. But to take the next step in automating you now also must learn how to use APIs and JSON. So, my ultimate tip for the future will be really getting to know the Invoke-Webrequest PowerShell command.

And as always with automating, if you must do something twice it's already worth automating it.

*An example PowerShell API call to get a login token – one of the most commonly used API calls –* *see next page.*

```
$login = "$uri" + "/Automation/API/Auth/Login"
$json_token = @{'userName' = $Username; 'password' = $Password}
$json_token = ConvertTo-Json $json_token

$token = Invoke-WebRequest -URI $login -Method POST -Body $json_token -ContentType 'application/json' | ConvertFrom-Json
$token = $token.token

if(!$token) {

    write-error "Could not connect to the API. Please check username, password and uri."

}else{

    Write-host -ForegroundColor GREEN "Succesfully signed in token is $token"

    Set-Variable -Name Token -value $token -Scope global
    Set-Variable -Name Uri -value $uri -Scope global
}
```

***Submitted by:***

**Name:** Hans Last **Country:** Netherlands **Job role:** ICT Specialist **Company:** Agrifirm

in www.linkedin.com/in/hans-last-201480b0

**Automate the boring stuff first – Power BI**

Everyone involved in IT knows something about writing reports. Managers love them especially, though administrators hate to make them. I would like to share how we automated this *boring* piece of work. Time and time again it saves us a ton of boring copy & paste work. The manually created version of the report contains a lot of high-level performance information from most of the components in our environment. For example, Service Management, Windows Updates, Backup and a lot more. Some tools are SaaS-based, while others are placed on-premises.

We saw the light when we got some insights into Power BI. Power BI is capable of integrating with almost any kind of data source. Some applications or tools also offer API or OData support. For other tools and information we have written PowerShell scripts to extract data and save it to a CSV file.

For this task we implemented Ivanti Automation to fully automate it. To transfer the information to Power BI in the Microsoft Cloud we installed the Power BI on-premises Gateway and connected it to our Power BI environment up in Azure. Now that all the required information is available we formatted and filtered the data to bring it into the graphical overviews.

The latest and greatest part of this job is to bring all the graphics together in one or multiple dashboards. The information is refreshed on a daily basis and the dashboard(s) is/are available to everyone who needs the information and at the moment they want it.

***Submitted by:***

**Name:** Trond Eirik Haavarstein **Country:** Brazil **Job role:** CAO – Chief Automation Officer **Company:** Xenappblog

 www.xenappblog.com

 @xenappblog

We're moving to the Cloud whether we want to or not: just look at how Office 365, Azure AD and MFA have become the de facto standard. Now that Microsoft and their partners start to push Windows Virtual Desktop, the SQL Server workloads will follow automatically.

For those of us who have been around for some time, remember the days of Server-Based Computing (SBC) where the rule of thumb was to keep the data close. Fast-forward to 2019 and the same is going to happen once again.

Which means that EVERY organization needs to invest even more money (not less) in training to prepare their IT organization for what comes next. This includes Cloud Management, PowerShell, DevOps and WinOps Automation, to name just a few. Another very important task is to also change the regular mindset about IT.

***"I cannot highly enough recommend the book:* The Phoenix Project: A Novel About IT, DevOps, and Helping Your Business Win.** ***Organizations failing to do so will fall behind their competition or even worse, go completely out of business. I would even go so far as demanding all my employees read it and an exam to verify."*** – Trond E. Haavarstein

So how do you get started?

That's why I provide the Automation Framework Community Edition free of charge and constantly publish new Evergreen Download and Install scripts on blog www.xenappblog.com & www.github.com/haavarstein

***Submitted by***:

**Name:** Tom Gamull **Country:** US. **Job role:** Solutions Architect
**Company:** Red Hat

in www.linkedin.com/in/magicalyak

www.magicalyak.org

@magicalyak

If we are doing something more than twice, we should automate. This is the common saying for answering the question of whether we should automate a task. However, often I've found that you may end up spending more time automating than doing the task as xkcd famously pointed out – see image below.

I always look to the time it takes to deliver as a key piece for automation, which means I measure before and after I automate. The number of times I am likely to repeat this task is also a good metric. My point is that I use a measurement or metric as my basis for automating, not just automating anything for any reason.

If you're looking to get started I highly recommend Ansible if you've never coded, or Puppet and Chef if you have some experience. PowerShell is also great for the windows side. Packer and Terraform are also great for multiple platforms. Also please use a version control system to store your scripts and automation: GitHub is a good start, even if you're new to it all.

**"Be the Automator, not the Automated."**

– Trond E. Haavarstein

***Submitted by:***

**Name:** Shane O'Neill **Country:** Ireland **Job role:** Engineer Advisor
**Company:** CVS Health

www.linkedin.com/in/sasponto

www.citrixtips.com

@SasPonto

**Automate. Automate. Automate.**

I cannot stress that enough. Two things can very quickly go wrong with Cloud deployments: sprawl, and inconsistency of standards.

If multiple teams are all let loose in your control plane GUI and they all start to spin up their own infrastructure items, you can be certain that they are all going to be doing different things from each other and you will have immediately lost control of any application of standards across your environment.

And then, over time, your inventory will have lots of orphaned resources with names like "temp-vm" or "test-storage" and these will add to your running costs overhead.

By instituting an Infrastructure as Code process to automate your resource deployments, you can prevent this from happening. By using this approach, you can ensure that required standards are enforced in all deployments in your Cloud environment.

As your usage of it matures, you will find yourself building up a library of reusable templates and blueprints that will allow you to very rapidly deploy new resources or scale out existing ones so the initial time investment in creating the templates will pay off in the long run. It will also make meeting any audit requirements that you need to adhere to much easier.

Getting people to adopt the Infrastructure as Code mindset is not easy. You will get pushback from folks who have only ever known point and click as how they do their work; indeed, many may not even be comfortable working with whatever API is available for your deployment, so upskilling and user education will probably be required.

The true value will be understood by those folks once they see how powerful the approach is and how it will make their own lives so much easier. And it is worth noting that Infrastructure as Code is a key enabler for DevOps, so should always be implemented in those scenarios.

**"Is that person worth 4 times the number of reboots and 10 times the number of security patches? The answer might be yes, or the answer might be, as Don points out, that these are IT professionals. Pro-fess-io-nals. That means you pay them money. Professionals who know how to do a job professionally. So in the IT profession, we learn new things. If you didn't want to learn new things, you should get into lumber. There has not been a new tree in quite a long time."** -Jeffrey Snover

***Submitted by:***

**Name:** Hans Last **Country:** Netherlands **Job role:** ICT Specialist **Company:** Agrifirm

in www.linkedin.com/in/hans-last-201480b0

**Lessons Learned, Automation and AzureRM**

Recently I was co-working on automating stuff to deliver fully automated resources through Azure Resource Manager. We started out at a certain point but soon after, the case became bigger and bigger. Even though we finished the job successfully, after evaluating the process we found some things we can do better in the future and I would like to share some thoughts on this topic.

First and foremost, make sure to have a clear plan, don't start with the technical stuff. Start with thinking about what you want to accomplish and get the requirements clear.

Write some kind of (functional) design and check the way the functions work, the ones you want to use, that is. Understand the limitations: it will save you a lot of trouble during the build process.

Start small. It can be tempting to keep building and lose the requirements out of sight. Start in a very early stadium with proper testing and test all the scenarios you want to use the automated stuff for. When the scripts and components are not big it is very easy to change or apply lessons learned.

Apply the same naming convention over the whole service you are building. When you need to link or pass through variables, or data from, for example, PowerShell to JSON templates, it is a lot easier to work when the parameters have the same naming convention.

JSON templates are very powerful, but they're not meant to replace PowerShell. In fact, it's the opposite: when using a combination of JSON and PowerShell, it is very flexible. JSON templates are static but PowerShell delivers the flexibility around them.

***"Think about how to organize resources using resource groups. Some resource types, like Availability Sets, need to be placed in the same resource group."*** – Hans Last

So far, some of my lessons learned were about automation and Azure. I would like to wish everyone success with automating everything. It is possible!

**"The first rule of any technology used in a business is that automation applied to an efficient operation will magnify the efficiency. The second is that automation applied to an inefficient operation will magnify the inefficiency."**

– Bill Gates

***Submitted by:***

**Name:** Chris Twiest **Country:** Netherlands **Job role:** Principal Consultant **Company:** Detron

www.linkedin.com/in/chris-twiest-a2378186

www.workspace-guru.com

@TwiestChris

**DevOps, Automation and the digital desktop**

These days, vendors are using a more DevOps mindset when it comes to their products. The product is never finished and they release major and minor versions (updates) in iterations. A good example of this is of course Windows 10. So, let's take a look at the migration to Windows 10.

Traditionally you would start a new project team. You would have a kick-off, an inventory, functional and technical designs, implementation, technical and functional testing and then the new desktop environment will Go-Live. The project team will be disassembled and maintenance will be transferred to the regular IT department.

These kinds of projects usually go over time, over budget and one of the biggest complaints is the knowledge transfer between the project team and the regular maintenance department. That is because in a lot of companies these people are not working in the same departments.

More often than not a group of external consultants will be hired and put in a room somewhere together to do the project without any one of the internal IT department working on the project beside them. So now imagine trying to do this every 6 months (minimum) when Microsoft releases a new version of Windows 10.

And if you are using Citrix with it, the Current Release channel is every 3 months. So, what better way?

Well, try changing your mindset. Think of your desktop environment not as a finished service with an A to Z project. Think of it as a product which you keep improving. Don't create a project team to go from A to Z, but create a team of professionals who can create, maintain, improve and adapt the desktop and keep them together.

***"Release a desktop that just works as quickly as possible to your users and see the response from your users as positive (continuous) feedback. And put this feedback on a prioritized list (product backlog). This way you know what the users (customers) want/need the most in the desktop."***
– Chris Twiest

Of course, a big part of this is automation. If you create the first desktop (product) completely automatically with scripts like silent install scripts, then you can improve upon those scripts and just keep redeploying the product as new versions (Infrastructure as Code).

Think about using Git repositories for your code so that you can easily see the differences between versions (changelog). This way you are moving more to a DevOps kind of mindset. You go from IT project employee to a developer and I think this is the way forward.

**"Any roles involved in a project that do not directly contribute toward the goal of putting valuable software in the hands of users as quickly as possible should be carefully considered."** - Stein Inge Morisbak

**"Currently, DevOps is more like a philosophical movement, not yet a precise collection of practices, descriptive or prescriptive."** - Gene Kim

# Networking and protocols

***Submitted by:***

**Name:** DJ Eshelman **Country:** US. **Company:** Eshelman Enterprises

www.linkedin.com/in/djeshelman

www.ctxpro.com

@TheCitrixCoach

Mind the Gap

"We went to the Cloud, and it's slow! We added bandwidth and CPU and it's still slow!" When corporations declare a hybrid Cloud strategy with EUC workloads... there is a danger!

The problem is when your DATA DISTANCE between backend data and front-end execution is too long. The mistake often made here is thinking in terms of download and upload speeds.

But applications generally don't care about bandwidth, they care about speed (and no bandwidth is NOT speed). Even 2 ms of latency can cause an issue with many applications because the number of *transactions* often number in the thousands.

Further adding to the issue is most TCP transactions require acknowledgement, making the overall transaction latency for data typically well over 5 ms or more when processing is involved. 5 ms latency isn't a big deal when downloading an MP3.

But 3000 transactions? Now let's look at a database hosted at 60 ms 'away' from the hosted desktop. Let's be generous and say there's no jitter and no processing. 120ms*3000=360000/60=6000 seconds! While you hope this is a worst case... I have seen it! Often the hosted desktop is blamed. Or the backend. Or bandwidth. But the solution is to always keep your *data* with your *execution*.

If you can't – Cloud may not be for you. If you can't get the data in the Cloud – you're usually best keeping the Resource VMs in the same datacenter. Sometimes this may mean splitting the difference between multiple PoPs to lower the distance between, but mind the gap!

***Submitted by:***

**Name:** James O'Regan **Country:** Ireland **Job role:** Cloud Architect **Company:** Hexagon PPM

www.linkedin.com/in/southcirc

@jamesoregan

One of the most important considerations for the Cloud is a stable and resilient network connection because this is crucial in determining end-user experience.

There are main factors that need to be considered including

- Bandwidth
- Latency
- Jitter
- Resilience

While connectivity levels are increasing there are still minimum levels required: for example, Netflix requires 1.5 Mbps for streaming now while most people have this. I have seen areas, for example in South America, where the connection speeds are below this limit. In areas such as these, access to the Cloud is simply not possible.

Latency has a huge impact on Cloud experience, so it is always vital in determining if the location is viable for Cloud access. Latency is the distance from the location to the Cloud Data Center with the desire to have the lowest latency possible. An example of this test is available at Azure Latency.

For example, my latency from my nearest Azure datacenter is 15 Ms which means I should have a good user experience because I have low latency and high bandwidth.

Jitter is defined as the variation in network latency: this again is another factor in user experience and another measurement that you want to have a low figure for.

Resilience is a huge factor with the Cloud because if you have issues with network access you will have either performance issues or no access. To combat this, we have a rise in usage on SD-WAN which allows you to combine multiple network links like, for example, combining a DSL connection with a couple of 4G connections and this increases your resilience; if one connection fails then the others take over until the link can be repaired

***Submitted by:***

**Name:** Trentent Tye **Country:** Canada **Job role:** Citrix Technical Expert **Company:** ControlUp

in www.linkedin.com/in/trentent-tye-367469b

www.theorypc.ca

@trententtye

The three most important words: latency, latency, latency.

When moving to a Cloud you cannot overlook the latency. Cloud providers try and prevent latency by having datacenters spread across the globe, trying to put them in areas where they can service the most people.

**Sponsored content**

IGEL is the world leader in providing software-defined endpoint optimization and control solutions for Cloud and virtualized workspaces. The company's world-leading software products include the IGEL OS™, IGEL UD Pocket™ (UDP) and Universal Management Suite™ (UMS).

These solutions comprise a more secure, manageable and cost-effective endpoint management and control platform across nearly any x86 device.

Easily acquired via just two feature-rich software offerings, Workspace Edition and Enterprise Management Pack.

Software presents outstanding value per investment. Historically known for its German-engineered Thin Client hardware, IGEL is now recognized as a leader in deploying a simple and secure, read-only Linux-based operating system which can be managed with ease via the Management Suite.

The operating system comes with over 80 integrated technologies including Lakeside, deviceTRUST, Cherry, Login VSI, Avaya, and more. The IGEL Cloud Gateway extends this management to remote, non-office-based endpoints.

IGEL supports Citrix, VMware, Parallels, and will offer support for Amazon workspaces and WVD in 2019. IGEL is also a Citrix Ready partner and regular sponsor of community events like CUG and VMware user groups. The IGEL community also now has over 1500 members: www.igel.com

But you may still have to deal with the ultimate killer of performance, latency, even with these attempts. Government organizations may have regulations stipulating that data is not allowed to leave the country. For a business in Vancouver, that means your nearest Azure datacenter is 2,090 miles away in Toronto, which means your ***fastest*** latency is in the 50ms range.

Characterizing where the data is generated from and where the data needs to be sent and whether the process is blocking is critical to get customer buy-in. An example is an application that blocks the user interface during the scanning of a document until the data is validated that it's safely stored at the destination.

Latency, in this example, can cause such a poor experience that it can kill your project before it starts. This requires creativity to mask the delay or vendor buy-in to modify their process or product. Or a closer datacenter. Of all the challenges in a Cloud-based world, latency is a physical limit that cannot be reduced. Light can't travel any faster. It's fundamental. Always consider latency.

**"Thirty-nine years of my life had passed before I understood that Clouds were not my enemy; that they were beautiful, and that I needed them. I suppose this, for me, marked the beginning of wisdom. Life is short."** – Imani David

***Submitted by:***

**Name:** Marius Sandbu **Country:** Norway **Job role:** Cloud Architect **Company:** EVRY

 www.msandbu.org

@msandbu

Many new SaaS-based solutions such as Office 365, Google G Suite are using PoPs (Points of Presence) around the world to provide low-latency connections to their service, in combination with GEO-based load balancing to provide optimized routes to the end-users.

To provide a good end-user experience it is crucial that the local network is optimized for internet traffic (Window Scaling, MTU Size, browser with support for modern network mechanisms such as TCP Fast Open, TLS 1.3 and HTTP/2). DNS is local to the client.

It is also important that SaaS-based traffic from an end-user on a remote location is using local breakout on each site and not routed back to the main office.

Also, that traffic is optimized from the endpoint to the Cloud using some form of network optimization such as SD-WAN. Many SD-WAN vendors provide packet optimization and can also provide packet flow across multiple ISP connections to load balance but also provide packet deduplication and other optimization of packet flow to ensure a better end-user experience.

Some vendors also provide SD-WAN-as-a-Service to optimize the entire packet flow from client to a Cloud service to ensure better end-user experience.

***Submitted by:***

**Name:** Bart Jacobs **Country:** Belgium **Job role:** Consultant
**Company:** BJ IT Comm.V.

www.linkedin.com/in/jacobsb

@CloudSparkle

**Get the (network) basics right.**

### "*Creating a movie starts with a script. Building houses starts with a plan. So should your journey to the Cloud.*" – Bart Jacobs

When creating that script, runbook, plan ... or however you would like to call it, don't forget to start with the basics. And in terms of the Cloud, always start with the network. Without a connection there's simply no point in using the Cloud. Get your network team involved early, not at the very end. Also make sure everyone understands you're all on the same side. You still very much need network engineers in a Cloud world. And what is the first step beyond your basic connectivity? Right, DNS. Without DNS... well, you can only memorize so many IP addresses. A slow DNS will slow your Cloud.

A slow DNS will get you and your users into trouble at one point or another. Evaluate your DNS resolvers and forwarding design, test, test, and then test again, and make sure to repeat those tests every now and again.

***Submitted by:***

**Name:** Rody Kossen **Country:** Netherlands **Job role:** Consultant **Company:** PQR

www.linkedin.com/in/rody-kossen-186b4b40

www.rodykossen.com

@R_Kossen

**The Future is (Hybrid) Cloud, just don't forget about connectivity**

So, you probably are working on a plan to move to the Cloud or trying to transform applications into SaaS. Even better, your plan is all done, and you are already utilizing Cloud services. But does your plan contain a chapter about connectivity? Did you think about what happens if your connection goes down because the roadwork around the corner destroyed your nice and fast fiber connection? Or how to connect your branch offices all around the world to your Cloud services?

So why not just add another line? Will you just add it as a backup and pay for, uh, just having it? In a traditional situation you would need to think about and configure a lot of things to make your connectivity high-available. Things like routing, failover scenarios and perform failover tests. But in a modern world you don't want to be occupied by these things, it just needs to work.

**Connectivity should be always-on, so make it software-defined!**

Luckily the solution can be found in creating a software-defined layer on top of your WAN connections, and SD-WAN was born. With SD-WAN you can use all your connections Active / Active, so you can utilize every connection you pay for and aggregate their bandwidth. Also, no less importantly you can make sure that the right data gets the right priority by using a QoS engine which identifies all your applications.

SD-WAN is delivered by many companies like Citrix, VMware by VeloCloud, Fortinet or Juniper. The concept is the same for all the vendors but, as always, the devil is in the details, so really look at what your requirements are and select the proper vendor for you. Most of the companies also provide the option to install SD-WAN on the major Cloud platforms (Microsoft Azure / Google Cloud, Amazon AWS) through the Cloud providers' marketplace as a Bring Your Own License (BYOL).

**But what about SaaS?**

With SD-WAN you can make smart decisions on how to route your traffic. If your policy is to backhaul all traffic to your datacenter to filter it by your corporate firewall, this is no problem with SD-WAN. But if you use SaaS services like Microsoft Teams or other latency-sensitive services this can be an issue as backhauling adds extra latency.

Luckily you can create simple rules so SaaS traffic will break out directly at the branch to lower the latency and enhance the user experience. Some SD-WAN providers even use the new Microsoft Office 365 API to route the traffic to the closest or best datacenter, so when the datacenter around the corner has issues you can still access your Office 365 services.

**Utilizing Cloud as a network provider**

Last summer Microsoft introduced Azure Virtual WAN as a new service, which is a next step for Cloud networking. With the global presence of Microsoft with their datacenters (45+!) and their many peering and front-door locations, there is almost everywhere quick access to their network.

With Azure Virtual WAN you can connect your branches to your datacenter or to another Azure region, so users can access the resources hosted on that region, by utilizing the Azure Backbone. Which is, I think, one of the most advanced and fastest networks in the world – see the image on the next page.

**"Everything is going to be connected to Cloud and data... All of this will be mediated by software."** – Satya Nadella

But wait, it gets even better. SD-WAN solutions utilize the Azure Virtual WAN API, so you only fill in your Azure subscription details in SD-WAN and create the hubs in your Azure Portal. After that, the API configures all the connections and routing for you.

I hope more Cloud providers will follow Microsoft's example and open up their backbone to customers, so it really makes it easier to connect to Cloud services in different regions.

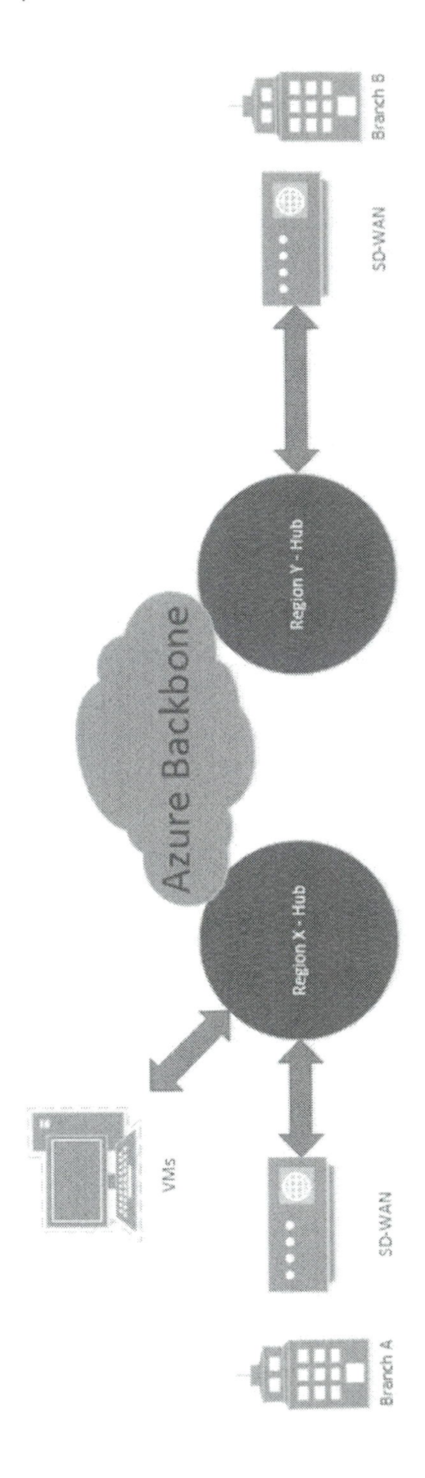
Branch B
SD-WAN
Region Y - Hub
Azure Backbone
Region X - Hub
VMs
SD-WAN
Branch A

***Submitted by:***

**Name:** Cláudio Rodrigues **Country:** Canada

www.blog.wtslabs.com

@crod

You have heard of GSLB. For sure. And if you are in the EUC – which I believe is the case, otherwise you would not be reading this – it is probably thanks to Citrix that you have heard of the term 'GSLB'.

If you are not aware, Azure does provide a very cheap and easy to use way to create a much more powerful GSLB solution, thanks to its traffic manager feature set. Using your own PowerShell scripts, you can flip users from one datacenter to another based on any sort of metric you may have in mind, way more flexible than a traditional NetScaler GSLB solution.

Definitely worth investigating it. If interested, check this blog post at http://blog.wtslabs.com/?p=91.

***Submitted by:***

**Name:** Leee Jeffries **Country:** Great Britain **Job role:** Consultant/Managing Director **Company:** Leee Jeffries Consulting

www.linkedin.com/in/leee-jeffries-0021752a

www.leeejeffries.com

@leeejeffries

When designing architecture in a Cloud-based environment it's extremely important not to overlook the same technical challenges that should also be considered on-premises.

Networking is a key part of any environment but specifically bandwidth and latency when we are talking Cloud. When you are moving workloads to a Cloud-based environment it's of paramount importance to ensure that your clients are able to access their workloads in the best way possible.

***"Consider where your users are based and ensure that the region being used to host your infrastructure is in the same location. Test connectivity, ensure that there is not a high amount of latency between your end-users and the target platform."*** – Leee Jeffries

Consider using a Virtual WAN-based solution to enable visibility and manageability to even the simplest types of internet connections. Virtual WAN enables full traffic control and analysis and helps to troubleshoot issues you may experience with connectivity.

***Submitted by:***

**Name:** Anton van Pelt & Patrick van den Born **Country:** Netherlands **Job role:** Senior Consultant, **Company:** PQR

www.linkedin.com/in/antonvanpelt

www.linkedin.com/in/patrick-van-den-born-2b3567a

www.antonvanpelt.com

www.patrickvandenborn.blogspot.nl

@AntonvanPelt

@pvdnborn

**Virtual Machine SKU sizes**

When deploying a virtual machine keep an eye on the maximum network interfaces that are supported for that particular SKU size. For instance, the D2s_v3 virtual machine size can only have 2 network interfaces assigned. This makes sense when you try to scale down the virtual machine size because it is not using all the resources.

**Network Security Groups**

Network Security Groups are meant to create a basic access control list for inbound and outbound traffic.

- A Network Security Group is not a firewall
- Network Security Group rules are stateless
- Always deploy a firewall to perform layer4–layer7 management and monitoring

By default, for each networking interface for the virtual machine template that you deploy via the Azure Marketplace a Network Security Group will be created.

You can imagine when there are 100 or more virtual machines deployed this will become a mess. The advice here is to create network security groups per network segment or VLAN rather than per virtual machine.

| PRIORITY | NAME | PORT | PROTOCOL | SOURCE | DESTINATION | ACTION |
|---|---|---|---|---|---|---|
| 100 | NS_SNIP_to_XDDC_STA | 80,443 | TCP | 10. .204.14... | 10. .204.10... | Allow |
| 200 | NS_SNIP_to_LDAP_LDAPS | 389,636 | Any | 10. .204.14... | Any | Allow |
| 300 | NS_SNIP_to_DNS | 53 | Any | 10. .204.14... | Any | Allow |
| 400 | NS_SNIP_to_NTP | 123 | Any | 10. .204.14... | Any | Allow |
| 500 | NS_SNIP_to_RADIUS | 1812,1813 | UDP | 10. .204.14... | 10. .204.1[illegible] | Allow |
| 600 | NS_SNIP_to_SF_HTTP_HT... | 80,443 | TCP | 10. .204.14... | 10. .204.37,... | Allow |
| 700 | NS_SNIP_to_VDA_ICA_SE... | 1494,2598 | TCP | 10. .204.14... | 10. 153.0/24 | Allow |
| 800 | Webserver_to_backend | 443 | TCP | 10. .204.99 | 10. .153.66 | Allow |
| 65000 | AllowVnetOutBound | Any | Any | VirtualNetw... | VirtualNetw... | Allow |
| 65001 | AllowInternetOutBound | Any | Any | Any | Internet | Allow |
| 65500 | DenyAllOutBound | Any | Any | Any | Any | Deny |

## Azure Load Balancer

If you want to make an application highly available you need the Azure Load Balancer functionality. Azure Load Balancer is a service within Azure that can be used to make servers and applications highly available. Even when deploying a Microsoft SQL failover cluster you need to deploy the Azure Load Balancer service.

Additionally, you can make use of an Application Delivery Controller like Citrix ADC, F5 BIG-IP or HAProxy. But this ADC needs to be fronted with an Azure Load Balancer. The reason for this is that Azure don't support floating IP addresses. It is not possible to create a highly available ADC solution without making use of the Azure Load Balancer service in Azure.

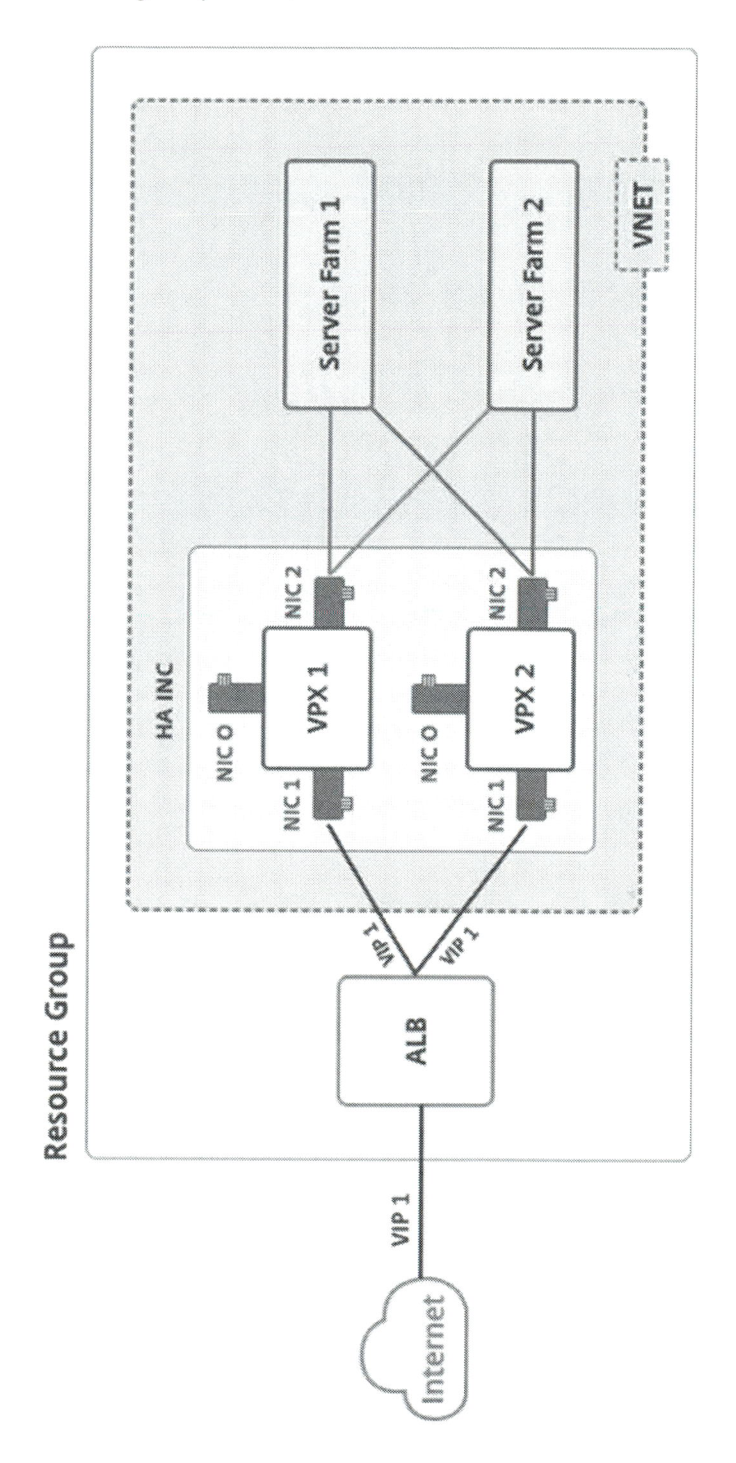
Resource Group
VNET
Server Farm 1
Server Farm 2
HA INC
NIC 2
NIC O
NIC 1
VPX 1
NIC 2
NIC O
NIC 1
VPX 2
VIP 1
VIP 1
ALB
VIP 1
Internet

**"Imagine a world where everything that can be connected will be connected – where driverless cars talk to smart transportation networks and where wireless sensors can monitor your health and transmit data to your doctor. That's a snapshot of what the 5G world will look like."** – Ajit Pai

# Costs

***Submitted by:***

**Name:** Mike Nelson **Country:** US. **Job role:** Architect

www.linkedin.com/in/nelmedia

www.geektweakers.com

@nelmedia

Don't be blindsided by the infamous public Cloud "sticker shock". Many folks who do not have a lot of experience in the public Cloud don't understand or realize the costs associated with consumption of public Cloud resources such as storage, compute, and bandwidth.

Although these costs over time are almost always less expensive than on-premises solutions, most people don't see their internal bills for resources, so they really have little concept of what those costs really are. It is imperative that you learn to use tools to constantly and consistently monitor, alert, and adjust your Cloud consumption usage.

In Azure, use Cloudyn and the Resource Usage and Billing tools. In AWS, use Budgeting and Billing tools. And in GCP, utilize Stackdriver, reporting, and labels.

There are many third-party tools or even ones you may have developed in-house. Also, use cost calculators when planning workload migrations and Egress operations such as DR failback, image copies, or transactional transfers.

Even with these tools, you must be diligent in monitoring and being keenly aware of your current Cloud costs, as well as changes in pricing for resources. These price fluctuations happen frequently in the public Cloud with changes in infrastructure and features. Stay alert, be aware, and keep those costs under control!

***Submitted by:***

**Name:** Scott Osborne **Country:** US. **Job role:** Sr. Solutions Architect/Regional Lead **Company:** Choice Solutions

www.linkedin.com/in/scottosborne1

 @VirtualOzzy

I guess first and foremost for me is that if you are thinking 'public' Cloud, don't go into the venture thinking you can take the same on-prem thought-processes, procedures, workloads, etc. and simply put that in somebody else's datacenters (GCP, Azure, AWS, etc.) and "save" money.

These Cloud players which include these big three as well as any other co-lo or hosting provider are providing at the most basic level IaaS and have to make money from this.

Unless you are able to completely eliminate your datacenter presence and the maintenance that goes along with that by moving to them, you will most likely have to figure out other ways to save money; it will be more about capitalizing from the other benefits of using the public Cloud.

The hybrid Cloud scenario is what most will be looking at for quite some time as the Cloud concept is all about flexibility, open APIs, consumption-style costs, etc.

Secondly, from a design standpoint, if there is one thing at the 101 level I can't stress enough, it would be to not forget about availability zones. Your IaaS provider will not be responsible for that – you will! They will patch as they need to do and you will be responsible for having that 'anti-affinity' concept built into your infrastructure workloads.

***Submitted by:***

**Name:** Anton van Pelt & Patrick van den Born **Country:** Netherlands **Job role:** Senior Consultant, **Company:** PQR

in www.linkedin.com/in/antonvanpelt

in www.linkedin.com/in/patrick-van-den-born-2b3567a

www.antonvanpelt.com

www.patrickvandenborn.blogspot.nl

@AntonvanPelt

@pvdnborn

The costs for Azure IaaS virtual machines are divided into monthly and micro costs. If you deploy a virtual machine from the marketplace the machine will cost you an X amount of dollars per month. So monthly costs are mainly compute and storage.

On top of the fixed price per month you also have to pay for the micro costs. Micro costs are disk IO / IOPS and also the network bandwidth that flows outside your Azure region, e.g. via an ExpressRoute or VPN Gateway to your on-premises datacenter.

**Cloud Sizing**

When sizing your Cloud environment, you have to think differently than when deploying an on-premises environment. The on-premises environment is mostly sized on the maximum capacity that it needs to handle. The IaaS sizing in Cloud environments, however, is based on the minimum/average need.

You can scale up whenever additional resources are needed. From a cost perspective it is also important that you start with small SKU sizes and proactively expand resources. You can easily upgrade an IaaS virtual machine to a different SKU with more resources when needed.

### Monitoring

When you've decided to start building an infrastructure on a Cloud platform we advise you to create a cost prediction forecast first. This will give you insights into the average costs you can expect. Microsoft offers several tools that will help you to monitor your resources both active and proactive:

- Azure Advisor
- Azure Cost Calculator
- Azure Cost Management (Cloudyn)

You can also make use of third-party tooling like CloudHealth. With CloudHealth you're able to do a 'what if?' comparison from a cost perspective. 'What if?' example: "What will my on-premises workload cost when moving to Azure or AWS?"

### Azure Limits

Azure does have default limits and maximum limits. The maximum limits are basically the max you can get out of the platform per subscription. If more than a maximum limit, an additional subscription is needed. Default limits, also named quotas, will protect you from deploying too many resources at once. For instance, by default each Azure subscription is limited to a total of 20 virtual machine cores.

In practice, it is very likely that more than 20 virtual machines cores are deployed in a subscription. Default limits can be expanded via a support case. Most of these limit support cases are processed automatically and expanded instantly.

Azure subscription and service limits are described in this Microsoft documentation: https://docs.microsoft.com/en-us/azure/azure-subscription-service-limits

You can check the current quotas per subscription by browsing in the Azure Portal to: subscriptions > usage + quotas.

| QUOTA | PROVIDER | LOCATION | USAGE | |
|---|---|---|---|---|
| Network Watchers | Microsoft.Network | West Europe | 100 % | 1 of 1 |
| Total Regional vCPUs | Microsoft.Compute | West Europe | 16 % | 56 of 350 |
| Standard DSv3 Family vCPUs | Microsoft.Compute | West Europe | 9 % | 32 of 350 |
| Standard DSv2 Family vCPUs | Microsoft.Compute | West Europe | 3 % | 10 of 350 |
| Storage Accounts | Microsoft.Storage | West Europe | 2 % | 6 of 250 |
| Standard BS Family vCPUs | Microsoft.Compute | West Europe | 2 % | 8 of 350 |
| Standard FSv2 Family vCPUs | Microsoft.Compute | West Europe | 2 % | 6 of 350 |
| Static Public IP Addresses | Microsoft.Network | West Europe | 2 % | 3 of 200 |
| Public IP Addresses | Microsoft.Network | West Europe | 0 % | 4 of 1000 |
| Network Security Groups | Microsoft.Network | West Europe | 0 % | 19 of 5000 |
| Availability Sets | Microsoft.Compute | West Europe | 0 % | 7 of 2000 |
| Standard Storage Managed Disks | Microsoft.Compute | West Europe | 0 % | 55 of 25000 |
| Load Balancers | Microsoft.Network | West Europe | 0 % | 2 of 1000 |
| Virtual Machines | Microsoft.Compute | West Europe | 0 % | 26 of 25000 |
| Virtual Networks | Microsoft.Network | West Europe | 0 % | 1 of 1000 |

### Personal Best Practices

- Some best practices we learned during several Azure projects are:
- Small disk images: by default, billing is based on fixed sizes of managed disks. These costs are based on tiers (32GiB, 64GiB, 128GiB, etc.). A standard image template from the Azure Marketplace is deployed with an 127GiB OS-disk. For Windows Server 2016 11GiB is initially used, so you will pay for 116GiB of air. By searching [smalldisk] within the Azure marketplace you'll find several Windows Server image templates. When deploying those templates, you can specify the size of the disk you need. Pay attention to the limited IOPS!

- Azure Reserved Instances: If you deploy a permanent workload that needs to run for one to three years you can make use of Azure Reserved Instances which will save you up to 72% costs compared to standard on-demand, pay-per-use Azure virtual machines
- Build a PoC with Azure B-series: B-series are burstable virtual machines. Burstable virtual machines are ideal for workloads that do not need the full performance of the CPU continuously. You will bank credits which can be used when full performance is needed at peak moments.

**"Cloud is just somebody else's datacenter."**

– Patrick van den Born and Anton van Pelt

***Submitted by:***

**Name:** Carl Stalhood **Country:** US. **Job role:** Principal Architect

in www.linkedin.com/in/carl-stalhood-73540724

www.carlstalhood.com

@cstalhood

The initial quote for Citrix Cloud Services is sometimes heavily discounted. When the first term expires, what is the price of the next term? Same discounts? Or will the price go up? If you don't pay for the next term, what alternative do you have to Citrix Cloud and how quickly can you implement that alternative?

If your goal is to put VDAs in Azure or AWS, you can simply add those Cloud-hosted VDAs to your existing on-premises CVAD implementation. It is not necessary to purchase Citrix Cloud-hosted Delivery Controllers just because you want VDAs in a public Cloud. You can even host your customer-managed Delivery Controllers and SQL in a public Cloud without purchasing any Citrix Cloud services.

**"If costs savings is your primary driver to consider, or adopt 'Cloud' you should rethink your game plan."**

– Bas van Kaam

***Submitted by:***

**Name:** Christiaan Brinkhoff **Country:** Netherlands **Job role:** Cloud Architect and Technology Evangelist **Company:** Microsoft

www.linkedin.com /in/christiaan-brinkhoff-18298740

 www.christiaanbrinkhoff.com

 @brinkhoff_C

The industry is going through the most extensive digital transition-transformation in our history. It tells us how fast we are going to leverage Cloud platform services. IDC – *Analyze the future* – reports that *"public Cloud IT infrastructure has more than doubled in the third quarter of 2018".*

**Source**: https://www.idc.com/getdoc.jsp?containerId=prUS44670519

Does this mean that the public Cloud will go mainstream in the next 5 years? I don't think so. Not every business is the same: enterprises particularly are different – in terms of application compatibility or consolidation, and short-distance needs.

It takes some time to get prepared for platform services, some apps must completely be rewritten for this reason. That's why not every public Cloud fits per use case right now. Requiring public Cloud services: due to a Cloud-first strategy or any other legitimate reasons results right now in a more hybrid approach before they (ever) will move entirely to a Cloud platform such as Microsoft Azure.

## ***"The Biggest Benefit of Cloud Computing is Lowering Costs."*** – John Doe

***Not so fast…*** The Cloud can quickly adjust the amount of computing power you're using, giving a lot of flexibility to your budget.

Focusing on cost – though – and not investigating how you might achieve significant efficiencies with new Cloud technologies after you could diminish your return on the Cloud investment, *is bad thinking if you ask me…*

Replacing on-premises workloads to Azure is not the key to success. I see it as a step – or better, a bridge – between legacy and “modern” applications. Success in the Cloud relies on the automated infrastructure around the server working well – it must save management and maintain effort as well as eventually benefit in costs.

The pleasure and fun about being active in information technology is to help customers to empower them in everything that they want to achieve. Doing the translation from on-premises workloads and/or traditional application to the Cloud can be bumpy.

The diagram on the next page helps me to explain the digital transformation to customers better – use it for your own benefit!

**"Besides using different platform services in the Cloud, always make use of reserved instances and power management tooling when leveraging IaaS Cloud infrastructures to make it more affordable for your business – when lift and shift is the only option."**

- Christiaan Brinkhoff

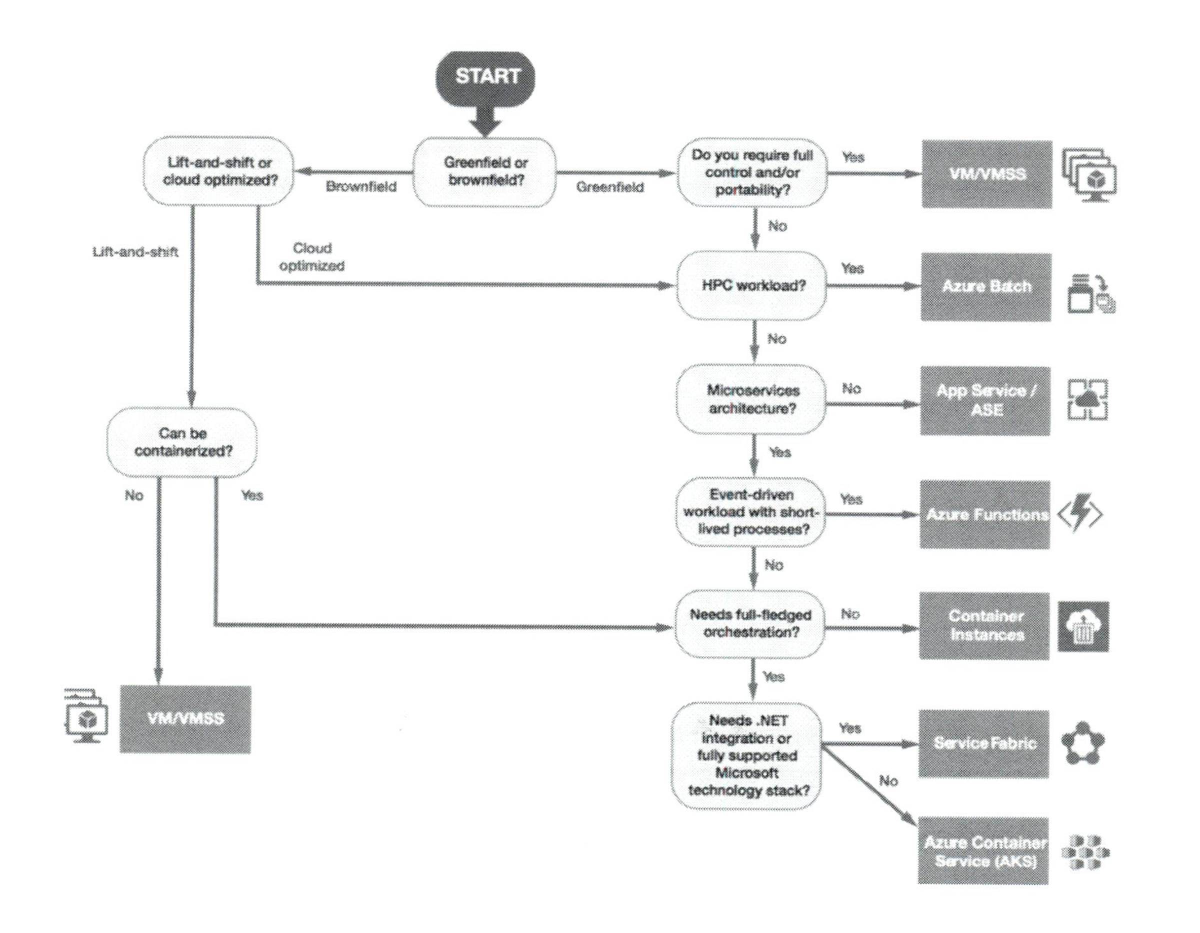
START
Greenfield or brownfield?
Brownfield
Greenfield
Lift-and-shift or cloud optimized?
Lift-and-shift
Cloud optimized
Can be containerized?
No
Yes
VM/VMSS
Do you require full control and/or portability?
Yes
VM/VMSS
No
HPC workload?
Yes
Azure Batch
No
Microservices architecture?
No
App Service / ASE
Yes
Event-driven workload with short-lived processes?
Yes
Azure Functions
No
Needs full-fledged orchestration?
No
Container Instances
Yes
Needs .NET integration or fully supported Microsoft technology stack?
Yes
Service Fabric
No
Azure Container Service (AKS)

***Submitted by:***

**Name:** Dave Brett **Country:** Great Britain **Job role:** End-User Computing (EUC), VDI, Cloud and Mobility SME

www.linkedin.com/in/dbretty

 www.bretty.me.uk

 @dbretty

When people start out on their Cloud journey they always consider it an easy win. For example, you just put in some card details and boom – you have a new Virtual Machine. The issue with that is there are so many hidden costs and complexities that are not even considered.

***"So many times have I seen companies struggle down the line when poor investment is made into the basic design and layout of their Cloud presence, be that fully Cloud-driven or hybrid. Start with the basics, region, network, storage, access and work your way up to the Virtual Machines."***

– Dave Brett

The VM is always the last thing that should be considered if you want a highly available and cost-effective Cloud deployment. Doing this will not only enable you to be flexible and fast-moving (as you should be in this new "Cloud"-driven world) but will enable you to provide real metrics and feedback to your business when they want to on-board new services into your Cloud presence.

***Submitted by:***

**Name:** Bas Stapelbroek **Country:** Netherlands **Job role:** Workspace Consultant / Solution Architect **Company:** KPN

@hapster84

Housekeeping will become more important in the Cloud. Administrating, documenting, cleaning up old ‘experiments’ and solutions is key to keeping your Cloud costs under control.

***Submitted by:***

**Name:** Jo Harder **Country:** US. **Job role:** Cloud Architect **Company:** V+

www.linkedin.com/in/joharder

 @joharder

Cloud is based on rented resources, so the less the rent, the lower your cost. When architecting and maintaining a Cloud solution, keep a watchful eye for resources that can be turned off. There are 168 hours in a week, and typically only 40 in a working week or about 25% of the time.

While you most likely need to have basic computing functionality available during non-business hours, do you really need to have all your VMs available? For example, the number of employees that access intranet web servers on a Saturday afternoon are far fewer than those that access on a Tuesday afternoon. If you can curtail the number of Cloud resources available during off hours, you can minimize your cost.

***Submitted by:***

**Name:** Sander Noordijk **Country:** Netherlands **Job role:** Consultant **Company:** Login Consultants

www.linkedin.com/in/Noordijk

www.vespertine.nl

@SanderNoordijk

It's funny how we have come so far with our whole Cloud movement, yet we still find customers and IT personnel that focus on the biggest misconception in Cloud computing: "It'll be cheaper!

Let's lift and shift everything! We can start right now!" Although they aren't wrong in the last statement, they are going about it completely wrong. Not embracing the power of the Cloud by just picking up on-premises configuration and placing it in VMs in the Cloud is a very, very bad idea.

***"It won't be cheap if you plan on using the exact same amount of resources you would in the office building. What you want is to make use of all the smart features Cloud elasticity offers."***
– Sander Noordijk

Start small and scale up or down when needed, use automation to turn machines and workloads off.

Think of which VMs you will always need to be online and choose to pay upfront for them, further pressing down on the price. The Cloud is versatile, but if you hang onto the old way of thinking you will not reap its benefits and probably overspend, badly.

***Submitted by:***

**Name:** Brian Madden **Country:** US. **Job role:** EUC Office of the CTO **Company:** VMware

 www.bmad.com

@brianmadden

The Cloud is not cheaper. (And that's ok.)

Now that "the Cloud" has proven itself as a viable alternative for on-premises Windows desktop and app hosting, customers are excitedly talking about getting rid of their on-premises VDI and moving it to the Cloud.

***"But when you actually look at the cost per hour, per desktop, and then multiply that by all the hours you need those desktops to run, the Cloud can get really expensive!"*** – Brian Madden

That's because the value of the Cloud is not realized in a "1-for-1" swap with on-premises infrastructure. Rather, the real value of the Cloud is that is that you only pay for the resources you use, while you're using them. The Cloud is great for scaling up (or "bursting") as needed.

It's great for slight growth that doesn't justify all new architecture on-prem, or for specialized workloads (maybe a few users who need GPUs that aren't worth buying a whole Tesla rig for on-prem).

But generally speaking, the value of the Cloud isn't that it's "cheaper". Once you have that mindset, making the decision of what to put in the Cloud, vs. what to keep on prem, is much easier.

***Submitted by:***

**Name:** Dennis Smith **Country:** Netherlands **Job role:** Architect
**Company:** Gourami

in www.linkedin.com/in/gourami

www.gourami.eu

@SMSPassword

**Down with the TCO**

'The Cloud': I still have a rather skeptical attitude if I hear people talk about 'the Cloud'. From my point of view it is still some sort of popular word amongst policymakers in IT. I never use the term myself, but when I hear it I cannot let the chance pass to ask the people who use it to elaborate.

Tell me in your own words, what does 'the Cloud' stand for, what does it exactly mean? Usually, this is the start of a very interesting and a rather long discussion. They answer things like: 'You don't actually store your documents on your own computer, but somewhere else.'

Then I ask, 'It's like a server with network share?' 'No!' they reply. 'We don't own the server.' 'So it's like hosting?' This is usually where the tone of the discussion changes, and they try to explain that it is the future and that it lowers the TCO.

I've been working in IT since long before this word (Cloud) was introduced. And to be honest it looks like something that was going on for years. Before people started using the term 'the Cloud', there already were pay-per-use computer resources.

We also ran applications via the internet, AS400, RDP and ICA. But the phrase 'Let's bring it to the Cloud' seems to have some special flair to it, especially for policymakers in IT.

And I don't know why this is exactly. As if you have your IT managed by God Himself – after all, God also resides in 'the Cloud'. Does that mean that 'the Cloud' is merely a term used for marketing? 'Old wine in new bottles'?

If you ask me, for the bigger part it is. And I have not seen a lot of success stories where the TCO indeed dramatically dropped. There are also a lot of problems if you hire resources from several parties. There is no such thing as a 'universal Cloud connector', which enables the interchange of information from several providers.

But that does not take away that 'the Cloud' concept', or 'pay per IT resources as you need them', is a great and flexible concept. Not only from a customer's point of view, but also from a supplier's point of view.

***"You can offer your product in a more flexible way, so you might make it available for people who would otherwise not use your product at all. Sometimes you don't need to buy a car, you just want to go to the movies."*** – Dennis Smith

I've mainly seen medium and small business benefit from 'Cloud services'. For big companies, I still see a lot of challenges: connectivity, printing and other technical issues, legal problems, GDPR to name one, and rarely a drop in TCO.

***Submitted by:***

**Name:** Jan Bakker **Country:** Netherlands

Saving money never ever has to be the main reason to move to the Cloud. Always look for ways to make things easier, not cheaper.

***Submitted by:***

**Name:** Adnan Hendricks **Country:** Netherlands **Job role:** Cloud Solutions Architect **Company:** Microspecialist Consulting

in www.linkedin.com/in/ahendricks

@Microspecialist

Cost can sometimes be a huge factor in design decisions when moving to the Cloud. Companies should try to refactor and modernize their infrastructure instead of building traditional IaaS on their Cloud platform.

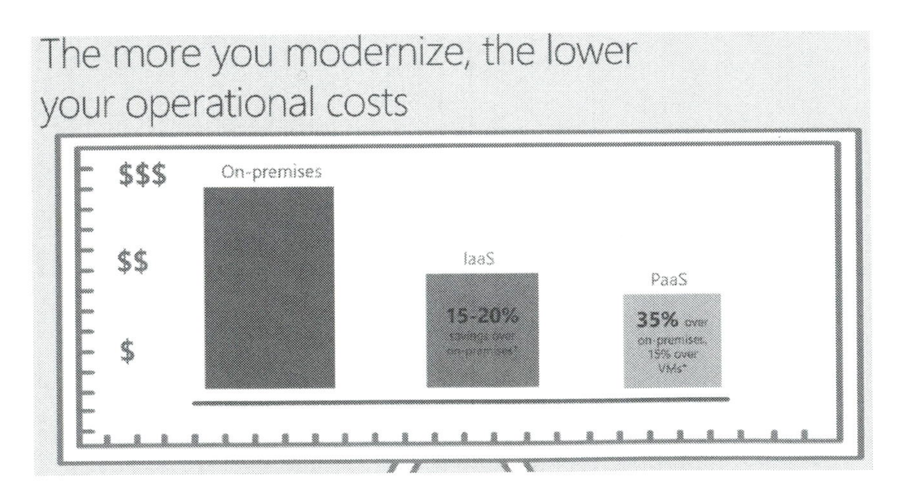

**"It has been proven that modernization and moving towards PaaS will lower the operational costs significantly. The second advantage in this process is that when the next evolution / migration of infrastructure comes along… for example, say a "microservices type architecture", they will then be able to move to that type of infrastructure much easier."** – Adnan Hendricks

# HA, DR & Backup

***Submitted by:***

**Name:** George Kuruvilla **Country:** US. **Job role:** Solution Strategist, Americas Pre-Sales and Worldwide Strategy **Company:** Citrix Systems

www.linkedin.com/in/gkuruvilla

www.blog.gkuruvilla.org

@gkuruvilla

I have had the good fortune of working at Citrix for nearly 7 years now and during that time, I've had the privilege of working with some of the largest and most strategic customers.

There is no denying that IT leadership across the board is now embracing the Cloud-first mentality. However, the fundamental challenge has always been finding the right use cases that would keep costs in check while also addressing the business challenges.

This is why I am generally excited to talk about leveraging public Cloud for disaster recovery (DR). When cost reduction is the primary driver, no other use case is a better fit in my mind. Most customers have a significant capital expenditure when it comes to DR, whether it's the active/active or active/passive model.

Customers have to invest in datacenters where the resources are rarely used, have to spend significant cycles trying to maintain the infrastructure in these datacenters and updating the software. This can be simplified significantly by leveraging the public Cloud.

So why public Cloud for DR? It's simple! Cost savings and flexibility. You no longer have to worry about the yearly CAPEX spend on DR infrastructure and maintenance of that infrastructure. Depending on your Recovery Time Objective (RTO) and Recovery Point Objective (RPO), you maintain the barebone compute in one or more of the public Cloud providers.

The goal being that in the event of a disaster, you can support a certain subset of users immediately and then use automation to spin up the additional workloads necessary to support all the users within the RTO. Even better, you are no longer tied to one provider. You have the flexibility of choosing resource locations across multiple public Cloud providers thereby constantly getting the maximum bang for your buck.

Moreover, it does not have to be a true IaaS solution. You could leverage PaaS offerings to further simplify the overall architecture, thereby managing both your production and DR environments with a single control plane.

This further simplifies the overall architecture, helps you take advantage of the latest and greatest features, and keeps the environment evergreen, thereby reducing the overall administrative costs and overhead. Thanks to the maturity of the public Cloud offerings, most offer solutions like Azure Site Recovery, and these tools can be used to back up and restore application backend and user data.

But how about user experience? That is of paramount importance! This is where industry standards like Global Server Load Balancing and leveraging a single FQDN front ending both the production and DR environments can really help.

Under steady state, when users visit the FQDN, they are taken to the production workloads, but in the event of an outage, they are redirected workloads running in the DR location. This provides a seamless end-user experience. So in short, one can reduce costs and management overhead without impacting user experience. What more can you ask for?

***Submitted by:***

**Name:** Adin Ermie **Country:** Canada **Job role:** Manager, Cloud Infrastructure **Company:** Avanade

www.linkedin.com/in/adinermie
www.adinermie.com
@AdinErmie

When planning and designing Business Continuity and Disaster Recovery (BCDR) for your applications/services, especially for Infrastructure-as-a-Service (IaaS) like Virtual Machines (VMs), it's not just the VMs you need to account for.

You need to account for all the other components and elements that support your Application/Service, like firewall rules, custom routes, load balancers, directory services, connectivity, storage, etc. It's "easy" to simply copy/failover a Virtual Machine; it's a lot harder to remember all of the lower-level supporting pieces that it relies on to make it work.

***"You don't want to find out during a disaster/failover that you missed/forgot a component."*** – Adin Ermie

***Submitted by:***

**Name:** Eric van Klaveren **Country:** Netherlands

www.linkedin.com/in/evanklaveren

www.euc-x.com

@EricvanKlaveren

When at a customer and the talk starts about (public) Cloud, a completely different approach is used as with an on-premises infrastructure. Security is the primary concern and placed high on the list. Aspects like Backup, Disaster Recovery and High Availability are forgotten.

Every situation is different, but the fact remains that what you pick are choices, responsibilities and should be motivated with – why?

Traceable back to the customer requirements, assumptions and constraints. I made a short list that helps me to make a choice for the customer:

- Why does the customer want to go to Cloud, identify the why and the need to migrate to the Cloud?
- The colors and flavors are enormous: does the provider fit the shoe (geographic, workloads, tools and APIs, etc.)?
- What payment options are there? How is it settled? (per hour, per day, per workload)?
- Which CSLAs are in place to guarantee capacity, availability and / or performance?
- Which laws apply to my data (workloads) and who has access or the rights to it?
- What about support, 24x7 and technical knowledge on support engineers?
- How is continuity guaranteed and which Disaster Recovery options are available?
- How is access secured and how is this monitored?

- Which network types, segmentation or protocols can I use, apply or create?
- What tools are available for automation, monitoring and orchestration?
- What migration possibilities are there from and to the service?
- On cancelation of the service, which steps are necessary? What happens to the data and information?

Of course, these questions are not everything you need to know, and each answer will raise new questions, but it is a good start!

**"You can have data without information, but you cannot have information without data."** – Daniel Keys Moran

# KEEP CALM AND ALWAYS ASK WHY

– Anonymous

***Submitted by:***

**Name:** Anton van Pelt & Patrick van den Born **Country:** Netherlands **Job role:** Senior Consultant, **Company:** PQR

www.linkedin.com/in/antonvanpelt

www.linkedin.com/in/patrick-van-den-born-2b3567a

www.antonvanpelt.com

www.patrickvandenborn.blogspot.nl

@AntonvanPelt

@pvdnborn

Like with on-premises resources, redundancy is very important. For example, running a web application that is hosted on multiple webservers, or a Microsoft SQL cluster. In an on-premises environment you make sure the workload is spread over different hosts. To cover the same functionality within Microsoft Azure we have to make use of availability sets.

**Availability Set**

In Azure there are no availability options on the hypervisor layer, such as HA, DRS or vMotion. When high availability for your application or service is needed, you need to arrange this at the application layer by deploying two or more IaaS virtual machines for that application.

Within Azure you add those virtual machines to an Availability set. Availability sets will ensure you having multiple virtual machines separated from each other on the Azure platform layer.

The platform ensures that in case of a failure not both or all resources are affected. This won't help when there is a failure in the entire Azure region!

Each virtual machine inside your availability set will get assigned to a fault domain. Virtual machines that operate in the same fault domain are making use of the same power and network resources. In the case where a power or network failure occurs, both virtual machines are not available.

By default, the virtual machines configured within your availability set are separated across up to three fault domains for Resource Manager deployments.

Also, each virtual machine inside the same availability set will get assigned an update domain. Virtual machines that have assigned the same update domain can get rebooted at the same time (forced by Microsoft by e.g. hypervisor updates).

Microsoft will ensure that only a single update domain is rebooted at the same time. When more than five virtual machines are configured within a single availability set, the sixth virtual machine is placed into the same update domain as the first virtual machine, the seventh in the same update domain as the second virtual machine, and so on.

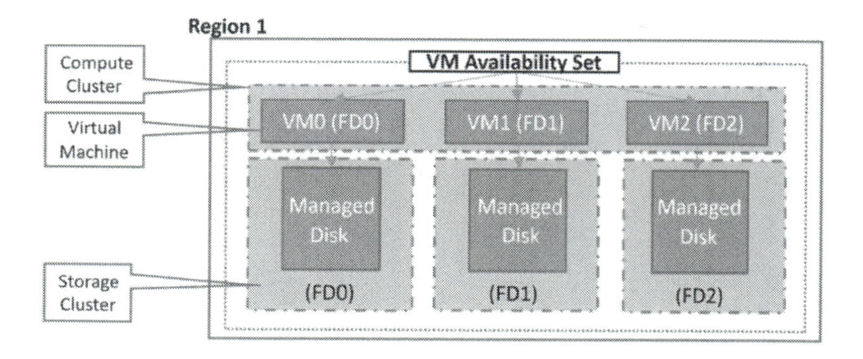

## Managed Disks

Microsoft recommends to make use of managed disks for IaaS virtual machines. The main reason for this is that when making use of unmanaged disks the VHD files are located within a storage account / storage blob. This storage account can run in another fault/update domain. In case of a failure or update there is a chance that the VHD will become unavailable and the virtual machine is still running.

When using managed disks, the VHD files are NOT located in a storage account and are located with the virtual machine, and thus in the same fault/update domain. At the moment Microsoft also recommends you to convert unmanaged disk to managed disk from within the Virtual Machine configuration.

Keep in mind to check whether the server you're deploying supports the managed disk configuration! If you still need to make use of unmanaged disks use separate storage accounts for each virtual machine that belongs to the same availability set (see availability sets). Also make sure that all disks (OS and data) that belong to the same virtual machine are in the same storage account.

You'll recognize managed disks by having the VHD file with the VM configuration:

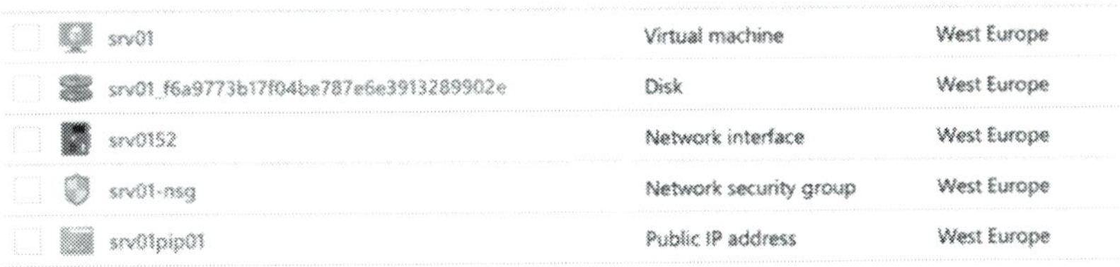

| | | |
|---|---|---|
| srv01 | Virtual machine | West Europe |
| srv01_f6a9773b17f04be787e6e3913289902e | Disk | West Europe |
| srv0152 | Network interface | West Europe |
| srv01-nsg | Network security group | West Europe |
| srv01pip01 | Public IP address | West Europe |

**Sponsored content**

As businesses mature in Cloud adoption, they realize a one-size-fits-all approach seldom works. They just keep getting better ROI and TCO when employing multi-Cloud-ready solutions like Parallels RAS, that leverage each Cloud deployment's strengths.

***"Parallels RAS makes it easy to deliver virtual applications and desktops from practically any Cloud – on-premises, public, hybrid, or even HCI (hyperconverged infrastructure)"***

Parallels RAS makes it easy to deliver virtual applications and desktops from any Cloud – on-premises, public, hybrid, or even HCI (hyperconverged infrastructure).

On on-premises deployments, acquire full supervision and control over your digital assets.

On public Clouds like AWS and Azure, get unlimited scalability, availability, and reach while avoiding huge upfront costs.

On hybrid Clouds, experience even greater business agility and scalability without compromising control where needed.

On software-defined, hyperconverged platforms, enjoy affordable Cloud-like capabilities minus a lot of the technical complexities.

Want to try a multi-Cloud-ready virtual application and desktop delivery solution for free? Grab a 30-day trial of Parallels RAS now

***Submitted by:***

**Name:** Harry Bos **Country:** Netherlands **Job role:** Senior Cloud Engineer **Company:** Uniserver

www.uniserver.nl

In today's public and private Cloud environments, high availability and other innovative solutions ensure that the availability in your environment is nearly 100%.

However, sometimes we have to fall back on the backup data. This can be through manual removal of important data, but also updates of a software package that ensures that the environment is no longer available. In some cases even a virus or malware outbreak.

The well-known method to ensure that the backup is set up properly is the 3-2-1 method. This 3-2-1 method stands for the following;

- 3 copies of the important date
- 2 different storage media
- 1 offsite location

With the above method, the backup is arranged in such a way that this data is available for every conceivable scenario. But this method lacks one crucial component.

Namely the validation of the backup data. You could have designed it so perfectly that the back-up data is always available. But without any validating of this data you can end up in a situation where literally ones and zeros are available without being usable for restore purposes.

To ensure that the backup data is usable, it is crucial to periodically perform an (automatic) restore test of this data, including its validation.

This can be done by testing basic functionalities whether the server responds to ICMP requests, or specific applications – for example, the SQL, Exchange instance is active. Or by executing specific scripts within an application – for example, an SQL query.

Just as important is registering the result automatically or manually. And if necessary, making adjustments to the production environment to achieve a successful restore result.

This way you will not be faced with surprises during a situation where back-up is your last resort. Backup must be a trusted service that can always be relied upon without any doubt.

# "It wasn't raining when Noah built the Ark."

– Howard Ruff

***Submitted by:***

**Name:** James Kindon: Australia **Job role:** Consultant **Company:** Insentra

www.linkedin.com/in/jkindon

www.jkindon.com

 @James_Kindon

When designing for Cloud HA, don't forget to account for the scenario where your application HA may well coincide with your provider HA.

Take, for example, the Azure Cloud platform and the concept of availability sets. Two servers in a single availability set ensure that your workloads are protected from Microsoft patching the underlying hypervisor, call them Production Node A and Production Node B. If one node drops (Node A), ideally the other node (node B) continues to serve operations as far as the availability set logic is concerned

But what happens when an application-level event occurs which off-lines Production Node A, whilst Microsoft decides to patch the node hosting your Production Node B.... (Citrix Cloud Connectors anyone?)

Key Takeaway – Availability sets in a 2-node deployment are not infallible.

# Performance and baseline

***Submitted by:***

**Name:** Kevin Howell **Country:** Great Britain **Job role:** Chief Technology Officer **Company:** HTG

www.linkedin.com/in/kevinhowellhtguk

www.htguk.com/blog

@kevhowla

Moving to the Cloud can be a daunting or an easy task depending on where you sit on the transformation journey. If you are working at a start-up, a green field setup is a dream, and consumption of services is a breeze (O365, Salesforce, Workday, etc.).

However, if you are working with an established organization, chances are that you will need to integrate with existing services which can be difficult to provide the desired outcome for both the business and the end-user.

Despite the benefits that Cloud can offer, I find it critical to run baseline checks on how the existing systems and applications are performing, along with taking time to understand how things are running for user (user experience tasks such as login, print, file access, application process tasks, etc.).

The reason behind this baseline is that on the journey to the Cloud, your business-critical data or services may no longer be contained within the same datacenter or connected over high-speed gigabit links as per previous best practice guides.

I have seen many organizations move or deliver some sort of project/service from the Cloud without understanding how that needs to integrate with existing services hundreds of miles away over high-latency links.

Often this ends up as a cross-vendor/supplier argument blaming various technologies and costing business considerable time and money.

Using a "baseline" will provide a measurable benchmark and alleviate any potential problems early in the digital transformation journey and may also prevent any potential blame game culture.

***Submitted by:***

**Name:** Eltjo van Gulik and Ryan Ververs-Bijkerk **Country:** Netherlands

 www.netwerkhelden.nl/cms

 www.logitblog.com

 @eltjovg

 @logitblog

Without data you're just another person with an opinion, especially in a Cloud environment.

In on-premises environments the latency is less of a problem compared to the Cloud in general. Regional locality has a big influence on the latency. Even in the Cloud performance needs to be measured to deliver the best user experience. Recent ICT-R research shows the performance perspective using Citrix Cloud.

***"Without data you're just another person with an opinion, especially in a Cloud environment."***
– Eltjo van Gulik & Ryan Ververs-Bijkerk

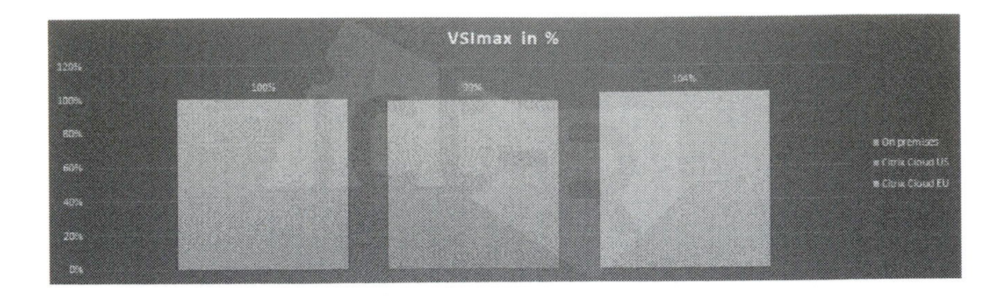


*Higher is better*

There is a small difference between the scenarios with a slight increase in the VSImax when using Citrix Cloud EU.

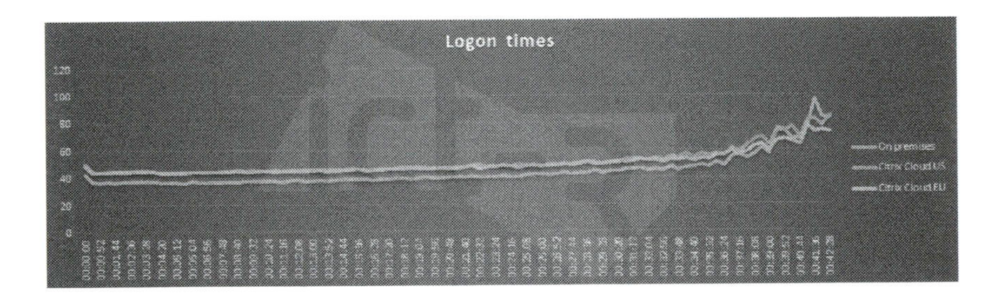


*Lower is better*

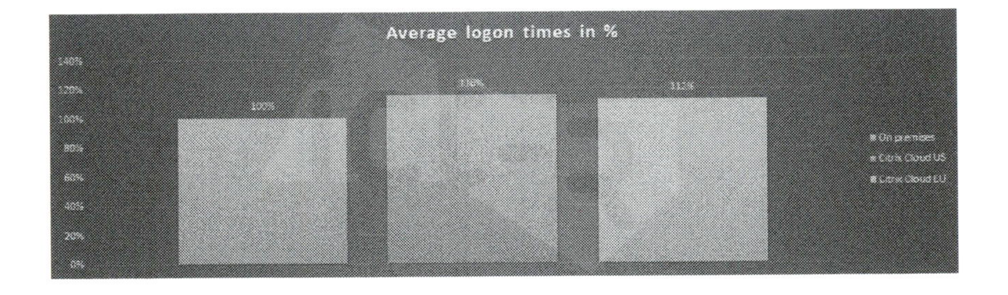


*Image – Lower is better*

There is an apparent impact on the user logon times. It is expected the US Citrix Cloud scenario takes a bit longer, as the distance to the datacenter is way further from our own datacenter.

With the average latency to Azure measured from http://www.azurespeed.com/ being around 150 ms to 200 ms to the West US and West Central US regions and the average latency to the West Europe latency averaging around 30 ms, some delay might be inevitable and the 12 and 16% increase in logon times is understandable.

Because Citrix Cloud is a PaaS offering there is less overhead on the infrastructure because most of the backend services will be handled to Citrix Cloud and do not require local servers to host them. This advantage will be even more apparent when using the StoreFront and NetScaler services of Citrix.

We expected the US Citrix Cloud offering to have a higher latency impact, with the US having only a slightly higher logon times compared to the EU.

We advise customers to always choose a region closest to their own location.

Full research can be found here: https://www.ict-r.com/using-citrix-cloud-from-a-performance-perspective/

This research shows that different regions influences the logon times, which is a big part of the user experience. Therefore, it is important to optimize and performance-test, especially in the Cloud.

***Submitted by:***

**Name:** Mark Plettenberg **Country:** Netherlands **Company:** Login VSI

www.linkedin.com/in/markplettenberg

www.loginvsi.com

@MarkPlettenberg

Performance in End-User Computing: it sounds so simple, yet many people are unhappy when it comes to the scalability or end-user experience.

In my opinion every admin for any environment, whether it's on-premises or in the Cloud, should be very strict on how they set up their storage, operating system, and – as the most common cause of performance problems – applications.

Here's some of the things I most often see misconfigured:

- Don't share storage with non-desktop platforms (e.g. SQL, webservers)
- Optimize your hardware settings in the BIOS: High performance!
- Validate the impact a GPU has on scalability
- Performance tune your operating system: VMware OSOT and Citrix Optimizer are easy, free and good!
- Think long and hard about workspace managers and anti-virus: if you don't configure them properly your users are going to suffer.
- Have a user profile strategy in place: roaming profiles are a thing of the past.
- Be critical on additional infrastructure components, application virtualization, layering: they add complexity and can slow down user logons.

- Be critical of every application that goes in. Do we really need it? Does it need to start at logon?
- Be in control, don't let other departments deploy software into your VDIs as if they are fat clients.
- Check your remoting protocol settings: do you really need 60FPS?
- "The Cloud" does not fix your performance problems, it just moves them.
- Using bigger instances in the Cloud is more expensive and does not guarantee better performance. Plenty of examples where the cheaper one outperforms.
- Finally: Measure everything, only make a change when performance goes up!

**"Never trust a computer you can't throw out a window."** - Unknown

**"Never let a computer know you're in a hurry."**

-Jeff Pesis

***Submitted by:***

**Name:** Dennis Smith **Country:** Netherlands **Job role:** Architect
**Company:** Gourami

www.linkedin.com/in/gourami

www.gourami.eu

@SMSPassword

Cloud performance

Cloud performance is a controversial topic. How are you going to compare Cloud providers, and particularly how do you guarantee that you are not measuring performance while one of the providers suddenly has a very busy moment. We all know that, especially CPU power, is overcommitted: some people call it oversubscribing. Meaning, if you order, say 100 CPU.

The Cloud provider puts your instance on a system that could handle '1000 CPU'. One would think you can host 10 of these '100 CPU' machines on that system. Wrong: on average people only use 5-10% of their assigned CPU power, and thus Cloud providers use this figure to 'oversell' their resource power. This is nothing new, and generally accepted. This not only goes for CPU, but also for network bandwidth and disk IO.

Desktop-as-a-Service (DaaS) is especially vulnerable for excess overcommitment and 'rush hours'. It's annoying that your webrequest on a web application takes 10 seconds, but working on a desktop where it takes 10 seconds for the Start menu to pop up is just plain unworkable. Nobody would want to work on this.

This is where the processor queue length comes in. Generally a Windows computer has more threads than available CPU cores, and this is where Windows queues the CPU tasks to have them handled by the next available CPU core.

Hopefully not all threads are active, and thus, hopefully, the CPU cores are able to process tasks quicker than they are coming in, and avoid them from getting queued. If this is not the case, and the Windows process must wait to get the attention of the CPU, things are getting sluggish. And this is called the process queue length, or PQL in short. If your PQL is off 0 for a long time, you won't be a happy DaaS user.

Products in general are known to have performance degradation. Suppliers generally will try to charge the same amount of money for an ever-degrading product. Who will notice that, over time, we put in 8 tomatoes in our soup instead of the 10 we had at the product launch when everybody said it was so rich in flavor.

Same goes for overcommitting computer resources from Cloud providers, who will notice that we overcommit from 200% to 250% or even 300% or higher. Your client's OS is also changing rapidly. Performance of Windows 10 version 1507 is not the same as Windows 10 version 1809.

So keeping an eye on the performance of your virtual desktops is a must. If the degradation goes slowly enough, people won't generally notice and complain about it. So measurement brings knowledge: make sure you measure on a frequent basis, and especially when conditions change.

***Submitted by:***

**Name:** Eric Kuiper **Country:** Netherlands **Job role:** Business Unit Manager **Company:** Salomon IT

www.linkedin.com/in/nlerickuiper

www.salomon-it.blog

When an employee has a bad user experience, he or she can become demotivated. I think we all agree that a demotivated employee isn't as productive and efficient as he or she could be.

The end-user experience is therefore of great importance, especially in Cloud-based environments with multiple moving parts and dependencies.

As an employer, it is important to know whether employees get the most out of their IT facilities. After all, if the user experience is poor – because of a sutured connection between the premises and the Cloud platform, for example – there is a chance that the employee will talk endlessly about this at the coffee corner, so to speak.

If you can come up with a way to constantly monitor and preferably quantify the end-user experience you might be able to take proactive measures. Besides that, you can use the information to create a baseline, which you can use for future reference. As I've learned throughout the years, there are multiple solutions that can help you with that.

In the end, this will help you to resolve incidents quicker, or even better, to prevent them. My tip would be to go out and give these types of solutions a try. You will have no problem in getting trial licenses, or (lightweight) support even, when you have questions or run into minor issues.

# Governance and SLA

***Submitted by:***

**Name:** Samuel Legrand **Country:** France **Job role:** Cloud Architect **Company:** LegSam Consulting

www.linkedin.com/in/samuellegrand

www.tech-addict.fr

@legsam59

**Cloud Service Level Agreement**

If you listen to the siren song from all "Cloud vendors", you will automatically think about how simple your daily job will be once you will be "in the Cloud". When talking about infrastructure, an important topic is availability.

Every vendor will tell you that its solution is "highly available": what does that mean? Service Level Agreements (SLAs) are available on vendors' websites. Let us have a look at two of them, VMware and Citrix.

Citrix Cloud objective is at least 99.5% monthly uptime (up to 3h39 of outage per month) where VMware Horizon Cloud is at least 99.9% (up to 44 minutes of outage per month).

Sounds good, doesn't it?

If you look at the terms of the SLA, you will see that for both, the "Regularly scheduled maintenance windows" for Citrix, or the "Scheduled maintenance windows where you have been notified at least 24 hours in advance" for VMware, are not considered as downtimes. Neither are "force majeure events"!

You should keep this in mind when giving your own SLA to your users or you can be in trouble!

***Submitted by:***

**Name:** Greg Shields **Country:** US. **Job role:** Author/Evangelist **Company:** Pluralsight.

www.linkedin.com/in/gregshields

www.pluralsight.com

@Concentratdgreg

Governance with Cloud services is easily Priority One in any successful implementation, and yet all too often it's the governance practices that are the afterthought. We've all heard the tales of the well-meaning developer who spins up the zillion-processor VM to run their database, only to incur a zillion-dollar bill at the end of the billing cycle. It's just too easy to do these things with Cloud services, and so making sure people _don't_ is part of the everyday care-and-feeding.

I sometimes argue that the term itself might be at fault. While "governance" is a valid vocabulary word, perhaps a better vernacular might be: "Are You Sure? Because This Costs Money!"

A term like that doesn't roll off the tongue like "governance" does, but it strikes to the root of the problem – even in the mind of that developer who really wants that supercharged database.

Some might argue, too, that governance (or, AYSBTCM for short) might just be the _entire activity_ that is Cloud services management. In the old days, my mantra to the uninitiated was: "In the IT world, developers are the folks that build things, and it's IT Operations that keeps them running."

That mantra is a little different these days. In today's universe of Cloud-enabled… Well, everything, my mantra might just be better stated as: "In the IT world, developers are the folks that build things, and it's IT Operations that keeps them _affordable_."

***Submitted by:***

**Name:** Michelle Gilbert **Country:** US. **Job role:** Solution Architect
**Company:** U.S. Bank

www.linkedin.com/in/michelleanngilbert

@michellesutopia

Cloud governance is key to evolving and transitioning in an evergreen service management model. As our organizations move out of a "traditional model" approach to reacting to change and into the "modern organization" we need to educate all of our stakeholders to learn and partner with future architecture and infrastructure decisions.

As an architect in Microsoft 365, we must remember that not everyone lives in the Cloud, and our efforts to build relationships have never been more important so we can help walk the path together, building the strength and foundation of our digital strategy as one to be the leaders of the future.

**"In SLA management, you think services, see SLA, hear SLO, perform SLA management."**

– Mussadiq Abdul Rahim

***Submitted by:***

**Name:** Jamil Talib **Country:** Great Britain **Job role:** Cloud and Automation Engineer **Company:** Aspen

www.linkedin.com/in/jamil-talib-b3a66985

 @jtalib

Governance of public Cloud in particular Azure should be one of the fundamental elements that should be prioritized for any Cloud journey. For techies, it is easier to get carried away by provisioning resources without the necessary controls around subscriptions. Cloud brings agility, flexibility and consumption-based pricing, and it is at this point that IT needs to put in the foundation for governance.

A well-thought-out set of practices and procedures like: Naming Conventions, Policies, RBAC (Role-Based Access Control), Tagging and Locks (to prevent resources being deleted accidentally) should be embedded in the Cloud strategy. Once these clear definitions have been attained, it is vital to set a Scaffold model, hierarchy and relationship throughout the Subscriptions down to any Resource Groups.

Another important element is setting and defining a chargeback (if your organization would do a chargeback model) for your Cloud consumption. Believe me, costs can ramp up if controls are not put around provisioned resources.

Consideration should be given to resources that are not needed to be on 24/7 and have an automated way of cooling down such resources. Think of Reserved Instance for such resources that are needed 24/7 (as business demands).

Fortunately, Microsoft have now made available a set of components and services within Azure that will aid and guide you in achieving this goal.

These components can be consumed as native packages of artefacts, policies that you define and apply as standards to resources in your environment and management groups for grouping and organizing subscriptions in a logical hierarchy.

**"If you think you've seen this movie before, you are right. Cloud computing is based on the time-sharing model we leveraged years ago before we could afford our own computers. The idea is to share computing power among many companies and people, thereby reducing the cost of that computing power to those who leverage it. The value of time share and the core value of Cloud computing are pretty much the same, only the resources these days are much better and more cost-effective."**

– David Linthicum

***Submitted by:***

**Name:** Rory Monaghan **Country:** Ireland **Company:** Algiz Technology

www.linkedin.com/in/rory-monaghan

www.rorymon.com

 @Rorymon

We have all worked in very reactive environments. Where the different departments were undersized, moved slowly on projects, and were in a constant battle just to maintain and support what was already there.

If that describes your current environment, know that yes, running some services in the Cloud can alleviate some of the workload BUT it doesn't necessarily guarantee that the service your end-users receive will be any more reliable or easy to support.

You'll see metrics with 98%-99% uptime. In reality, 2018 saw multiple high-profile public Cloud disruptions which raised the ire of customers.

Management should also be aware when these disruptions are occurring with these public Cloud services, getting answers and updates won't be as easy as walking down the hallway. A certain disruption last year lasted several hours and the status updates were only posted about every 2 hours. The root cause was also changed! Before jumping in, accept a lack of visibility and transparency.

**"There was a time when every household, town, farm or village had its own water well. Today, shared public utilities give us access to clean water by simply turning on the tap; Cloud computing works in a similar fashion. Just like water from the tap in your kitchen, Cloud computing services can be turned on or off quickly as needed. Like at the water company, there is a team of dedicated professionals making sure the service provided is safe, secure and available on a 24/7 basis. When the tap isn't on, not only are you saving water, but you aren't paying for resources you don't currently need."**

– Vivek Kundra

# Education

***Submitted by:***

**Name:** Jasper Kraak **Country:** Aruba **Job role:** Solution Architect/MCT **Company:** Inova Solutions

www.linkedin.com/in/jasperkraak

www.kraak.com

@jasperkraak

I'm a Microsoft Certified Trainer next to being a (Pre-Sales) Consultant. The biggest pitfall I see frequently is a huge lack of knowledge. Before you can even start to have a conversation on running workloads in a Cloud, make sure your customer knows what he/she is talking about.

We have done some successful experiments with giving away training for free as a pre-sales instrument. Then at least there is a starting point to talk about architecture.

***"The Value of your IT Investments is only as Big as you Train your Users (users include IT Staff)."***
– Jasper Kraak

So how funny does it get? I was invited by an IT manager recently to do a demo on Microsoft Teams. Stakeholders, business decision-makers, the IT manager and IT staff were present, and I did my thing for 45 minutes. The whole room was pretty excited! I delivered a good demo.

And then... the IT Manager asked me how to install that on their servers. I was totally unprepared for that question! I got away with it by saying that that was out of scope, a too technical story for now (I did not want to make a fool out of him in front of the room).

***Submitted by:***

**Name:** Tobias Kreidl **Country:** US. **Job role:** Systems Architect
**Company:** Northern Arizona University

in www.linkedin.com/in/tobias-kreidl-7ab249a3

@tkreidl

Whether or not to push applications into the Cloud is a complex decision in many cases, in particular if extensive on-premises infrastructure already exists.

Not only are there conversion issues to figure out, but also the burden of not only the migration, but also the sustaining of both local and off-site environments at the same time. There is the expenditure already made for on-premises equipment, which typically takes several years to be fully amortized. Hence, there will be the sometimes higher-than-expected costs of Cloud-hosting (especially if not scaled properly) to factor in, together with sustaining local costs.

The amount of human effort (time, training, added tasks) also has to be taken into account. In short, there are few good ways to reliably come up with the true costs. It's truly very challenging. Read a lot and ask a lot of questions. Starting small is smart. The Cloud option can be way more attractive if starting with nothing, since you can scale as needed up or down with no physical facilities to worry about.

Getting a good consultant can be a very valuable investment if you are not familiar with the intricacies of the process, and factoring in redundancy, disaster recovery and acceptable downtime should be done diligently. Be wise enough to know if backing out is the best recourse if things end up not going well enough; you can always revisit a full or partial migration (hybrid model) at some point in the future.

***Submitted by:***

**Name:** John Doe **Country:** The Lost World **Job role:** Creator of Things **Company:** I'd rather not say

www.google.com

Let me start by saying that I'm still new to all things Cloud-related. I'm slowly getting acquainted with the wonderful world of 'Cloud'. However, that doesn't stop me from discussion various use cases with customers and my direct colleagues.

Learn as you go and try to get as much hands-on experience as you can. Start out small and work your way up. Perhaps you can help out some colleagues, while educating yourself further, be mentored, ask for help when not sure – **just do it** basically. Even if it costs you a couple of bucks per month, next to what you can get for free at most Cloud providers, it will be one of the best investments you'll make.

**"Education is the passport to the future, for tomorrow belongs to those who prepare for it today."** – Malcolm X

Certifications are a *nice to have* and in some cases a *must-have* depending on the type of company you work for and how they do business. Just don't make them more important than they are. I would also recommend using CBT (Computer-Based Training) material, or online videos in general. YouTube, for example, has a ton of free and helpful stuff as well.

***Submitted by:***

**Name:** James Ma **Country:** US. **Job role:** Citrix Architect
**Company:** Cloudma

in www.linkedin.com/in/jameswma

@jameswma

Technical knowledge requirements for any job today have increases exponentially. Keeping up is now a full-time job in itself. There are no books that will give you the field knowledge of technology product and services, hence the need to learn from our peers.

There are many peers that are out there producing new content: we should not only be consumers of their content, we should proactively support this community. Join user groups and provide feedback.

***"Share what you know when you can, but what I think matters most is to share your questions, ideas and opinions. It will enrich all of us."*** – James Ma

***Submitted by:***

**Name:** Sander Bruijs **Country:** Netherlands **Job role:** IT Consultant & Practice Leader **Company:** SBC Solutions

www.linkedin.com/in/sander-bruijs-a4992510

www.comegetit.nl

**The New Kid On the Block**

I'm still relatively new to Cloud computing. I just earned my first few Azure certifications because I think Cloud computing is not only the future, it's here and has been for some time now.

I think most people don't even realize the scale of it but the adoption of the Cloud-based services we all know has been extremely seamless, which to me proves that the technology and its foundations are here to stay. Looking at it purely from the point of view of a system engineer, Cloud computing is the amalgamation of technologies like networking, storage and security and I find it exciting to be able to work with these technologies under one common denominator.

This has encouraged me to start discussing use cases with customers and my direct colleagues, and also to be part of a massive project for migrating users and mailboxes to the Cloud. I think it's important to learn as you go and coupled with the theoretical background this has been a perfect opportunity to get even more acquainted with the fundamentals of Cloud computing.

During my entire career I have been encouraged to think for myself but not to be afraid to ask. I guess this mantra also goes for more experienced Cloud specialists I have worked with because they have been able to really help me extend my knowledge on the topic. It's how we learn and help each other in a sometimes dog-eat-dog world.

Talk to your employer to find out if there's a Cloud-related project going on or coming up with which you can assist. That's probably the #1 way to develop your skill set.

I can tell from my own experience that it can work that way and it doesn't have to be a big project to begin with. Be it a hundred or multiple thousands of users or mailboxes or simply terabytes of BIG data, the basics and concepts remain the same in the end.

**"Lack of education, the problem is."** - Yoda

Even if it's in your own spare time, try to take the opportunity to improve upon your skills because don't forget, Cloud computing is fun! (That's at least partly why you're reading this book, right?)

***"In over your head? Make sure to carve the subject up into smaller sections or steps. That way you won't lose focus."*** – Sander Bruijs

Think of it as being a more agile approach: smaller sprints get you to faster results. Who cares if you need to change things around a couple of times or perhaps start over from scratch? You are learning, do not forget that!

**"Cloud computing is actually a spectrum of things complementing one another and building on a foundation of sharing. Inherent dualities in the Cloud computing phenomenon are spawning divergent strategies for Cloud computing success. The public Cloud, hybrid Clouds, and private Clouds now dot the landscape of IT-based solutions. Because of that, the basic issues have moved from 'what is Cloud?' to 'how will Cloud projects evolve?"**

– Chris Howard

# Miscellaneous

We had a couple of submissions that were not directly related to Cloud services, but are (more than) worth highlighting nonetheless. It's always going to be a fine line between on-premises, Cloud, hybrid, etc. Often it also depends on your point of view.

***Submitted by:***

**Name:** Rachel Berry **Country:** Great Britain **Job role:** Independent Consultant **Company:** Virtually Visual

www.linkedin.com/in/rachel-berry-74798bb

www.virtuallyvisual.wordpress.com

@rhbbse

Just buy your employees a dedicated mobile phone for work. The cost and hassle of doing BYOD are high and the risks if you do it badly are also high. Avoid the hassles of segregating work and home data and all the issues when someone leaves, who pays the bill, who replaces if lost/stolen on work business. It really isn't that much of a hassle to pop an extra mobile in your handbag, and for the guys there are some lovely man bags these days!

Some recent laptops have gained a little extra screen space by putting the camera down near the keyboard rather than above the screen. Avoid these as endpoints as it means everyone ends up on video calls with 13 chins and looking up nostrils. Check the camera is in a sensible place!

***Submitted by:***

**Name:** Cláudio Rodrigues **Country:** Canada

 www.blog.wtslabs.com

@crod

One thing most people in the EUC tend to forget is the simple fact there are way more vendors out there than simply Citrix and VMware. Many have simple, compelling and in many ways more polished solutions at a much lower entry price.

Next time you are working on a new EUC project make sure you take a look not only at the core platform, Remote Desktop Services (RDS) that is very capable for certain use cases and environment sizes, but also at vendors like Accops and Parallels.

***"After all, our main goal as EUC consultants is to deliver the right solution for the job. This means giving a hammer to someone that is using nails and not a screwdriver. Keep that in mind at all times. Right tool for the job. Always."***
– Cláudio Rodrigues

***Submitted by:***

**Name:** DJ Eshelman **Country:** US. **Company:** Eshelman Enterprises

www.linkedin.com/in/djeshelman

www.ctxpro.com

@TheCitrixCoach

Criteria for scalable & lower risk OU structure:

- Block Inheritance and use Loopback REPLACE.
- Link in only policies that are relevant and safe, re-creating those that need modifications to exist for VDI/RDSH scenarios.
- Avoid logon scripts. It isn't 1998.
- Think 2-3 years ahead with OU design.
- For the easiest control delegation and visibility for policies, use a widened OU structure instead of relying on filters.
- Begin with Baseline Policies, then use filtered exceptions for subsequent policies (e.g. allowing access to devices to specific user groups). Exception policies should only have the relevant settings, not a copy of the entire policy.

*Top-level domain*

- Citrix Infrastructure
    - Datacenter / Platform
        - Control
            - Controllers (Connectors)
            - Provisioning Servers
            - StoreFront Servers
        - Resource

*Baseline Policies*

- Desktop OS
    - Persistent
        - Machine Catalog (per OS)

*Computer Policies*

- Delivery Group (Use Case)

*(User Policies)*

- Non-Persistent
    - Machine Catalog (MCS – per OS)
        - Delivery Group
    - Device Collection (PVS – per OS)
        - Delivery Group
    - Server OS
        - Persistent
            - Machine Catalog

*(Computer Policies)*

- Delivery Group (Use Case)

*(User Policies)*

- Non-Persistent
    - Machine Catalog (MCS – per OS)
        - Delivery Group
    - Device Collection (PVS – per OS)
        - Delivery Group

***Submitted by:***

**Name:** Nick Casagrande **Country:** US. **Job role:** IT Director
**Company:** LGL Recycling LLC

www.linkedin.com/in/nickcasagrande

@virtualnickc

For VMs, be sure to remove any unnecessary hardware such as Serial Ports, Parallel Ports and Floppy Disk Controllers. This is especially true when building your VDI gold image to clone out 1000s of times.

***Submitted by:***

**Name:** Bram Wolfs **Country:** Netherlands **Job role:** End-User Computing Specialist

www.nl.linkedin.com/in/bramwolfs

www.bramwolfs.com

@bramwolfs

What EUC means for me

For me "End-User Computing" means the gathering and harmonization of all services that are needed to make end-users as productive as possible. The following 3 key elements play a crucial role in every End-User Computing solution:

1. The solution should support the organization's goals and ambitions
2. From an end-user perspective the solution should be easy to use and not limit productivity
3. The solution needs to be secure and flexible by design

With the above in mind, our goal as EUC specialists is to advice, implement and manage the best possible End-User Computing solutions for our customers.

And if you want to go a step further: The EUC industry has a very broad community and there are different platforms to share knowledge, hang out with like-minded people like yourself and above all to learn from each other!

***Submitted by:***

**Name:** Patrick Coble **Country:** US. **Job role:** Security Architect **Company:** VDISEC

www.linkedin.com/in/vdihacker

www.vdisecurity.org

@VDIHacker

*A few more from Patrick (he submitted multiple times). Make sure to check out his VDI Lockdown guide once it releases in May 2019.*

**Byte-Size Security Nugget – Privileged Access Management (PAM)**

Hacker Pro Tip = Don't log into anything other than Domain Controllers when you're a member of a Built-in Privileged group like Administrators, Domain, Enterprise or Schema Admins. Don't leave your privileged hash from these groups on your VDI Servers or Desktop images either.

In most IT departments Privileged Access is out of control based on the number of privileged accounts, the percentage of IT staff that have privileged access beyond what they need to do their jobs. Another major risk is that most users with privileged accounts use that same account to check their company email and browse the internet.
This is a huge risk to any organization no matter the size. A single computer infection can spread to multiple devices in your domain by just a simple phishing email that got clicked by a privileged user. Privileged Access Management can be handled at a couple of

levels, some are free, and some are not, depending on how far you want to or need to go. Below is a list of Privileged Access Management levels that range from some free best practices to what most of the third-party products can offer.

*PAM Level 1 – Free*

- Audit your default Built-in Privileged Groups like Administrators, Doman Admin, Enterprise and Schema Admin Groups. You will most likely find some surprises if you are not doing regular audits. I recommend doing this quarterly at a minimum.
  - In most organizations you only need 2-4 members in each of these groups with a couple of emergency service accounts only used in outage\lockout situations.
  - Set an Administrators, Domain, Enterprise and Schema Admin password expiration policy that is more often than your normal users. Privileged Account expiration shouldn't be every 90 days like most default user policies. Going back to only having a couple of Domain Admins you will find in most cases that the role may be relegated to just a couple of service and emergency accounts. The longer the amount of time between password changes, the higher your risk is to pass the hash attacks. You may also want to double the password length requirements, too.
- Remove inactive employees from any of the Built-in privileged groups.
  - This may also be a good chance to do a compare of your HR records and AD to find old employees that still have access, they may not be an Administrator, Domain, Enterprise or Schema Admin, but unnecessary enabled accounts are still a risk to your business, especially with most people reusing passwords for multiple accounts within their professional and personal lives.
- Audit your Service Accounts that were in the built-in privileged groups. Most service accounts do not need to be in those

groups. Proper delegation of administration can take time, but lowering the risk is worth it.

- VDI, SQL, File Server, Application Admins and many others do not need to be elevated to Domain Admin or similar built-in groups to do their jobs.
    - Make VDI-Admin, SQL-Admin and other groups as needed per job role along with groups of common server roles so that jobs can be aligned with access to this and that.
    - These groups can be applied to the Administrators group of each of these server roles. It is recommended to use Restricted Groups because it can help slow\prevent those groups from being removed from a Server role and there will be multiple audit logs if someone changes it.
- On your Session Hosts and/or Virtual Desktops images ensure your users are not administrators on these systems.

*PAM Level 2 – Free*

- All IT users that need privileged access must use a separate account: their normal account will have no extra permissions to the domain or other systems.
    - The Permissions necessary to do the Job role should be assigned to this separate admin account only.
    - Example username01, superusername, sausername, and others, in some cases you may want to obfuscate these accounts by using your standard to hide which accounts have these extra privileges.
    - Your built-in groups, Administrators, Domain, Enterprise and Schema Admins may also want a separate account just for those roles in some cases depending on their other responsibilities and the size of the organization. I would recommend further obfuscation if used: using another name may be helpful without any special designations to make them harder to spot.

- Once the privileged permissions have been separated from their normal Accounts, be mindful of where you log into with these accounts because of the hash it will leave behind.

*PAM Level 3 – Paid*

- Most Privileged Access Management Solutions have the following features.
    - They will have a Password Management system integrated so that privileged access is taken to the next level. This can allow a user account to perform privileged actions and the password is reset after use, each day or each session. With PAM systems like these the privileged accounts passwords are changed hundreds of times a year instead of just 1-4 times a year, which drastically reduces the attack surface and helps mitigate pass the hash attacks.
    - They have Session Management which means all the RDP and SSHs will funnel through this system and pass the credentials along throughout the process. This means you can give elevated access without the user ever having the password and also with having session limits and session recording.
- These sessions can be audited by recording them based on policies and they may also collect and/or correlate event logs and command line entries used to see what someone did while elevated.
    - They can change passwords after each account use or on a regular basis, too.
- There are many other design decisions related to a PAM solution and it will change the way you administer your systems, but it can also drastically reduce your attack surface when done right.

**Sponsored content**

Do you want to benchmark a large number of computers or servers? VDI Drones is a Windows Forms application and lets you specify and start CPU, Memory and Disk load on multiple machines at once. This is especially suited for benchmarking a large group of virtual machines under a hypervisor in VDI/SBC/DaaS situations. You can specify precisely how heavy the load should be in terms of threads, CPU, memory and disk.

Primary use cases:

- Verification of new infrastructure.
- Measure impact of changes.
- Testing of hotfixes & service packs.

Features:

- Enables load generation on a large number of machines.
- Easy to use GUI, no scripting skills needed.
- No need to set up hundreds of user accounts.
- Extremely easy and straight forward to install and set up.
- Specify the workload in detail, in terms of threads, CPU, Memory and Disk I/O.
- Integrates with your Microsoft Active Directory.
- Works on all major hypervisors: VMware, Hyper-V, XenServer, Nutanix and Microsoft Azure.
- Competitively priced licensing model.
- Available as a portable .exe, installation not required.
- No client side software installation required.

If you would like to learn more, go to www.vdidrones.com. VDI Drones is an www.gourami.eu company and a registered trademark.

- I would also recommend to not deploy a PAM without a multi-factor authentication system for all users that need privileged access.

## Byte-Size Security Nugget – Fault Domains

When designing any "IT thing" the first order of business is Safety First, which means making it highly available and then don't forget secure it and finally test it. Making things highly available is a great way to keep your job in the IT world and keep your users happy during maintenance windows or actual system failures. This is the process I have used to make almost anything more highly available.

*HA\Fault Domain Design Questions*

- Does the system support it?
    - Do you just need to just add a second system and they glue themselves together?
    - Does the system have a specific system like a cluster or something else to make it official?
- Will it require other systems to make it HA?
    - Most major products can take care of themselves when you add another instance or have a way to make it work.

**"In computer networking, a failure domain encompasses a section of a network that is negatively affected when a critical device or network service experiences problems. The size of a failure domain and its potential impact depends on the device or service that is malfunctioning. For example, a router potentially experiencing problems would generally create a more significant failure domain than a network switch would. Smaller failure domains reduce the risk of disruption over a large section of a network, and ease the troubleshooting process."**

– *Wikipedia*

- Then there are some systems that will need something to glue the network services like a load balancer.
- Then there are some systems that may also need shared storage between the two systems to make it highly available. This is when it normally gets more complicated.

- Local-Site Failover or Multi-Site Failover?
  - Single-Site Failover
    - If you have just one site to work with it may just require 2x servers instead of one and whatever it takes to glue them together.
  - Do you have multiple sites you must support?
    - If you do this may make things more difficult to finalize the design, whether the sites are two different buildings, two different datacenters, a datacenter and a Cloud provider or two different Clouds.
    - This is where a global load balancer may come into play for some systems to glue it together. You may also need to design your systems to have local-site and multi-site failover in mind.
      - 2 Servers in Site A, 2 Servers in Site B
  - Can both sites be active at the same time? In many cases the software may support servers\nodes spread between two sites in an active\active format, but maybe your application doesn't. In a VDI design you need to decide if you want to give someone a desktop that may not have all their working applications based on their limitations of failover plans, or just follow your failover capabilities with everything else. I would always rather have as much done for a DR failover than wait until the last minute and have more work to do.
  - Sometimes it may be better to have two separate deployments that do not know about each other. In the VDI world it could be a separate Site\Farm, and that the master images are replicated between them. This will increase your operational burden, but it may be worth it to

have two canaries in the coal mine. You can upgrade or change one without affecting the other.

- Datacenter Basics
  - Every Rack should have two separate paths to power.
  - Every Rack should have two separate paths to the Network
  - Every Server should have two separate network and power uplinks.
    - LOM\OOB uplinks in most cases are just a single uplink.
  - Split your deployment between Racks if possible. You may not have enough hardware or rack space to split it evenly between at least two racks. Split what you can and where you can so that a rack failure can be mitigated or at least softened.
    - When in shared spaces this may be not possible or cost-prohibitive, but I would suggest trying.

*Build for Failure*

- If you need 10 Servers for a workload, buy one extra server for N+1. Then, when you need the next cluster make sure and buy another extra server.
- If you have to have multiple clusters for a solution it may be good to split the clusters so you can do an upgrade before affecting a whole deployment. This can also keep you more operationally nimble so that you can do things faster, since a whole cluster can go down for maintenance instead of one server at a time. This usually only happens in large deployments but I have seen it justified in smaller deployments because of the benefits it can provide.

**Byte-Size Security Nugget – Top 10 GPOs**

When designing a VDI deployment there are lots of Group Policies to choose from to help lock down access, but it is highly recommended to at least start with these below because they give you the biggest bang for your buck. These are policies you will also want to "Deny" from applying to you so you can still administrate the system. Please test these settings before promoting into production.

1. Remove Run
    1. This is one of the most powerful settings that limit the user from doing so many things.
    2. GPO: User Configuration\Policies\Administrative Templates\Start Menu and Taskbar\Remove Run menu from Start Menu
2. Restrict CMD
    1. This is a great starter policy to limit administrative access.
    2. GPO: User Configuration/Administrative Templates/System/Prevent access to the Command Prompt
3. Restrict PowerShell Access (AppLocker)
    1. Most deployments do not block PowerShell, but it is even more powerful than the Command Prompt.
    2. GPO: Security Settings\Application Control Policies\AppLocker
        1. Select "AppLocker"
        2. Select "Configure rule enforcement"
        3. Select "Executable Rules", Check "Configured" (Which will be Enforced: you can just turn it to "Audit Only")
        4. Then Right-Click "Executable Rules" and Select "Create Default Rules"
        5. Right-Click "Executable Rules" and Right-Click and Select "Create New Rule"

6. Check the "Skip this page by default" and then Select "Next"
7. Select "Deny" for the Action and Select the "Select" button.
8. Enter an AD Group for this PowerShell Restriction and Select "Next"
    1. In some cases, it is recommended to create a group that you will then nest multiple Delivery or Entitlement Groups into. This will be done so you don't have to create multiple AppLocker Policies for each user group.
    2. I have also used AppLocker-No-PowerShell in a couple deployments as an example.
9. Select "Path" and then Select "Next"
10. Enter or Navigate to the following files and Select "Next"
    1. C:\Windows\System32\WindowsPowerShell\v1.0\powershell.exe
    2. C:\Windows\System32\WindowsPowerShell\v1.0\powershell_ise.exe
    3. C:\Windows\SysWOW64\WindowsPowerShell\v1.0\powershell.exe
    4. C:\Windows\SysWOW64\WindowsPowerShell\v1.0\powershell_ise.exe
11. At the Exceptions Select "Next"
12. Enter a "Description" then Select "Create" (Repeat this process on all 4 PowerShell Executables)
13. Allow the Policy to Apply and then Launch any of the 4 PowerShells and you should not be able to launch them while in the AppLocker group.
14. You can open the Event Viewer and Navigate to "Application and Services

Logs\Microsoft\Windows" and Select "AppLocker" then "EXE and DLL" to view logs.

1. You should see an 8004 Event Error if you have AppLocker Enabled to "Enforce Rules"
2. You should see an 8003 Event Error if you have AppLocker Enabled to "Audit Only"

4. Restrict All Drives
    1. Limiting access to browse the file systems can help prevent unauthorized access and, in some cases, some simple attacks can be blocked by this policy. You may also still need to use NTFS Permissions to limit access also if your application opens a path that you don't want users to be able to leave.
    2. GPO: User Configuration/Administrative Templates/File Explorer/Prevent Access to drives in My Computer
5. Restrict Help Programs
    1. Using Help is a very common Jailbreak method and depending on your application it may need more or less.
    2. GPO: User Configuration\Policies\Administrative Templates\System\Restrict these applications from being launched from Help
    3. Common EXEs
        1. iexplorer.exe,cmd.exe,regedit.exe,mmc.exe,powershell.exe
        2. There are many more: depending on what application your program launches you can prevent each one.
6. Remove Mapped Network Drives (Only Map drives if you have to)
    1. You should be mapping network drives for users and they shouldn't have the ability to map drives on their own in most deployments.

    2. GPO: User Configuration/Administrative Templates/File Explorer/Remove "Map Network Drive" and "Disconnect Network Drive"
7. Remove Control Panel
    1. Access to the Control Panel should be restricted.
    2. GPO: User Configuration/Administrative Templates/Control Panel/Enable -"Prohibit access to the Control Panel and PC Settings"
8. Remove Windows Installer Rights
    1. Users should not be installing new applications or processing Windows Updates.
    2. GPO: Computer Configuration\Policies\Administrative Templates\Windows Installer\Enable – "Prohibit User Installs"
    3. GPO: Computer Configuration\Policies\Administrative Templates\Windows Installer\Enable – "Prevent users from using Windows Installer to install updates and upgrades"
9. Remove Access to Regedit
    1. Access to the Registry Editor should be restricted.
    2. GPO: User Configuration\Policies\Administrative Templates\System\Enable – "Prevent access to registry editing tools.

***Submitted by:***

**Name:** Aaron Parker **Country:** Australia **Job role:** Solution Architect **Company:** Insentra

www.linkedin.com/in/aaronedwardparker

www.stealthpuppy.com

@stealthpuppy

If you're managing mobile devices, don't manage what you don't need to. Mobile application management (MAM), that allows you to control mobile apps and corporate information flow, will be much simpler to deploy and manage than the devices themselves (i.e. iOS and Android). MAM supports corporate-owned and personally owned devices with the same approach without requiring you to support device policies, complex testing and user-initiated device enrollment.

**"Mobile use is growing faster than all of Google's internal predictions."**

– Eric Schmidt

# Survey results

As part of our community approach we thought it would be helpful, and fun, to put together a small questionnaire on all things Cloud-related. Questions and statements on some of the most discussed topics throughout the last couple of years. VDI/DaaS, traditional (Windows) applications, reasons to leverage various Cloud services, or not, and so on.

The main idea was that by keeping the questions and possible answers reasonably short, this would lower some of the barriers people might have in contributing to this project. We fully understand that writing down a piece of advice, statement, recommendations, design principles, your thoughts in general, or whatever the case may be, is not for everyone. Next to that, it takes time, which, as most of you know as well, is a *rare* and valuable thing in our profession.

With this survey it became a whole lot easier to contribute – in a different way, sure, but a contribution nonetheless. So, the same applies here – a big thankyou to everyone who dedicated their time to go over these questions, even if it was only 5 to 10 minutes.

Throughout the next few pages we've collected all questions and statements including the answers and feedback we've received.

***Note that directly after the questions and answers, there is a section where we wrote down all 'Other' replies, on a per question basis. If a question isn't listed it means that there were no 'Other' comments posted, or that the option to leave a comment simply wasn't there.***

Keep in mind that with some questions/statements it was possible to select multiple answers. The survey was **filled in by 176 people. All numbers/answers are in percentages.**

## Survey summary

First off, we really enjoyed going through the 'Other' answers: some were serious, some were not, at least we hope so. You'll find them after the individual questions.

We're stuck with 'traditional' Windows applications for many more years to come. Some think they will outlast Twinkies even. And almost everyone agrees that Cloud in general isn't cheaper – far from it in most cases.

Hybrid and/or multi-Cloud deployments is/are the way forward, though it's clear that having a Cloud-first strategy/vision is seen as important by a large group – almost 57%. Next to that 41% thinks that Cloud only could become a reality within 15 years from now.

Current *traditional* VDI and SBC solutions still have their value and are not mainly kept alive for revenue purposes. As a result of this hybrid mix, a unified workspace portal of some sort is seen as critical by most – 70.5%.

It's clearly not the year of DaaS. On the other hand, most do believe that the upcoming Microsoft Windows Virtual Desktop release will have a big impact once it hits GA.

Also, the majority is already using some sort of DaaS solution or is at least thinking about doing so within the next 2 to 3 years. And by the looks of it, most will go with Microsoft's Azure platform as they are thought to be the biggest Cloud provider within the next couple of years, by far. Not surprising.

Latency, poor network configuration, and sutured connections are seen as a big threat to a successful DaaS deployment and/or Cloud use in general. Over 76% agree. This and data/app locality are also topics that are mentioned in the book multiple times. This is also where 5G networks might be beneficial in the (near) future.

**Q: Once released, the Microsoft Windows Virtual Desktop #WVD will have a major impact on DaaS going forward.**

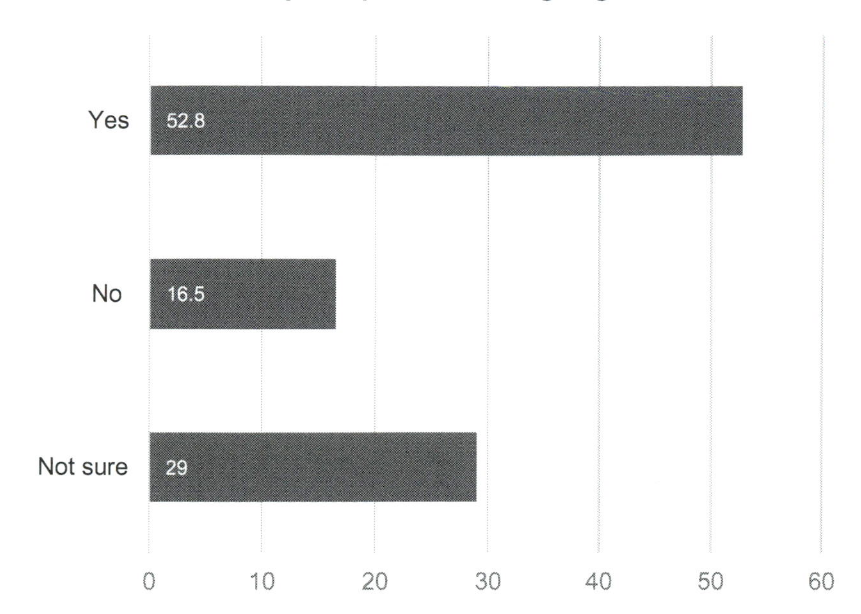


**Q: How important is a Multi-Cloud and/or Hybrid Cloud strategy for your DaaS (including future DaaS) environment?**

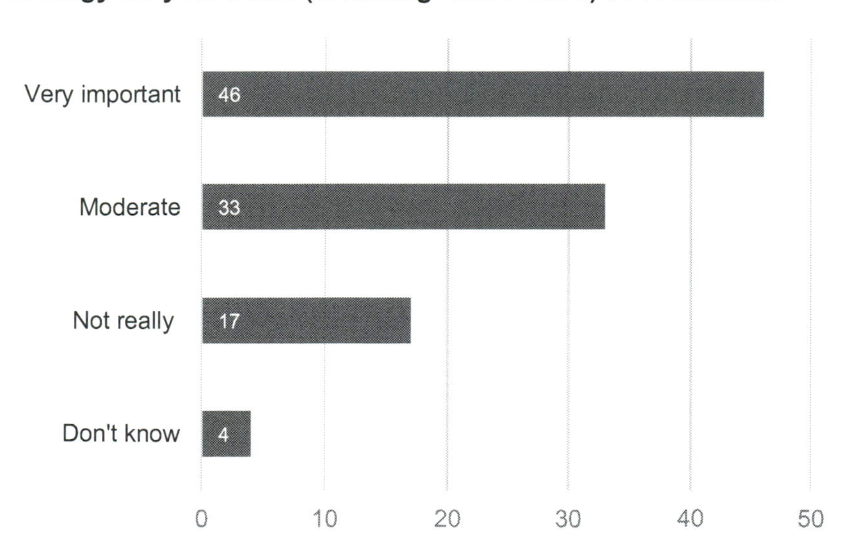

**Q: Traditional applications will be with us for at least…**

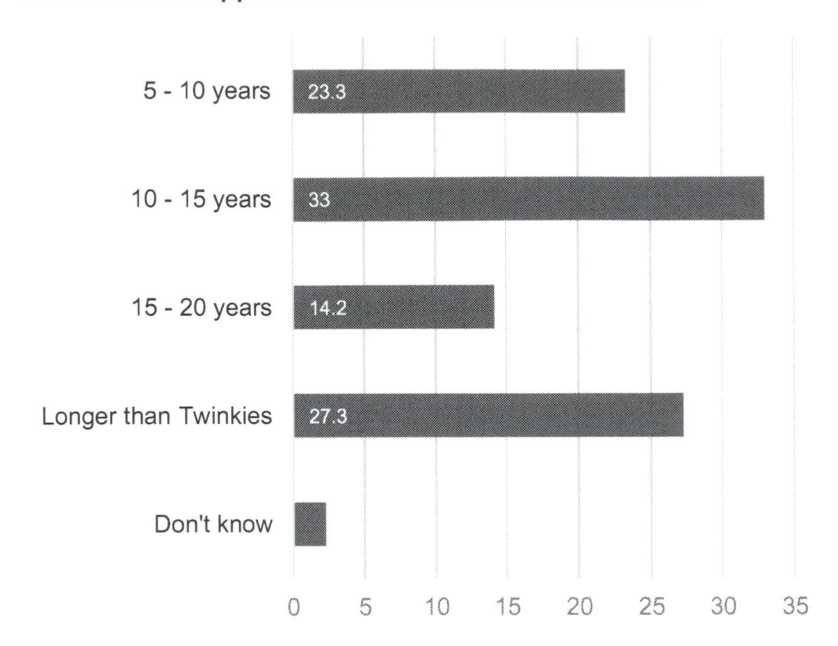


**Q: Is 2019 the year of VDI/DaaS?**

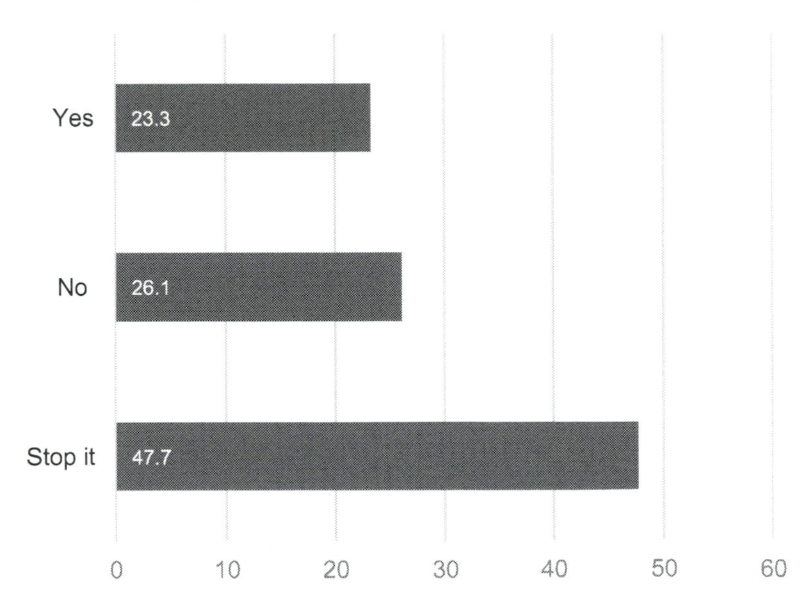

**Q: 'Cloud only' can become a reality within 10 to 15 years.**

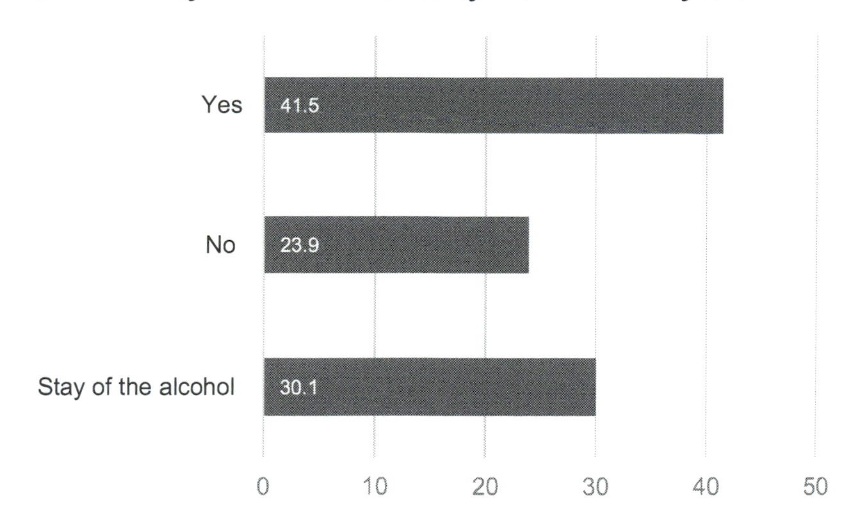


**Q: There's too much focus on Cloud-based workspaces and other EUC-related services. The true power (and future) of 'the Cloud' lies within other technologies and developments like BIG data, AI, VR and more.**

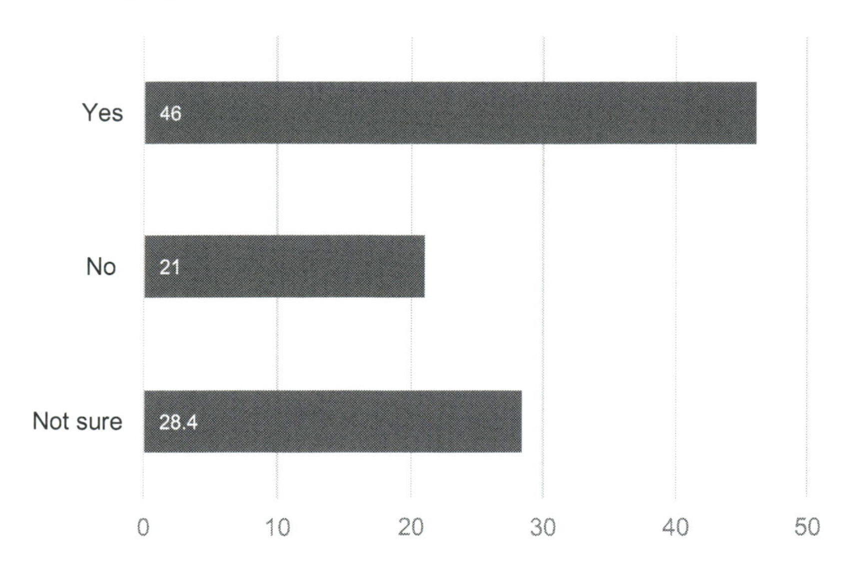

**Q: Do you see a need for a Unified Workspace Portal – one dashboard, a single pane of glass for all your virtual apps and desktops, SaaS, and Mobile applications, etc?**

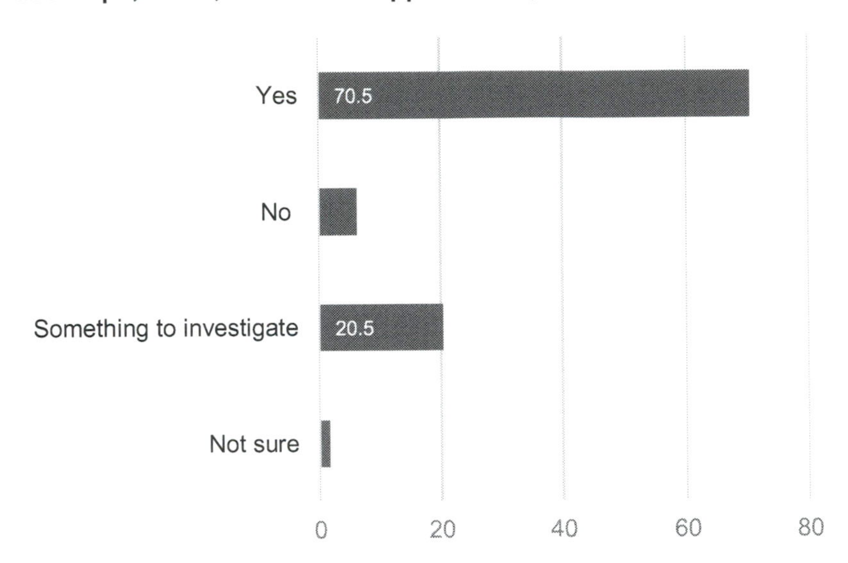


**Q: Latency, poor network configurations, and statured connections in general are some of the biggest threats to successful Cloud adoption.**

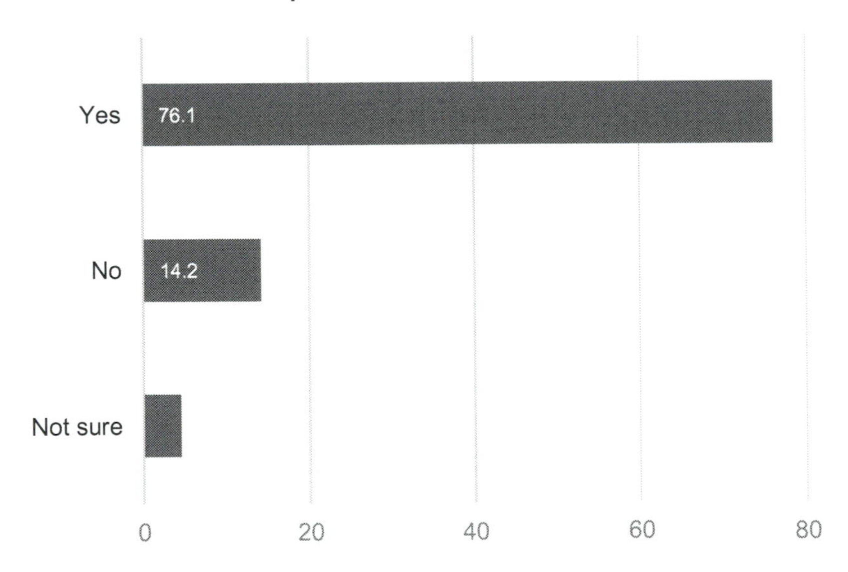

**Q: Do you think that the next Windows Server 202.x version will include the Remote Desktop Services (RDSH) roles?**

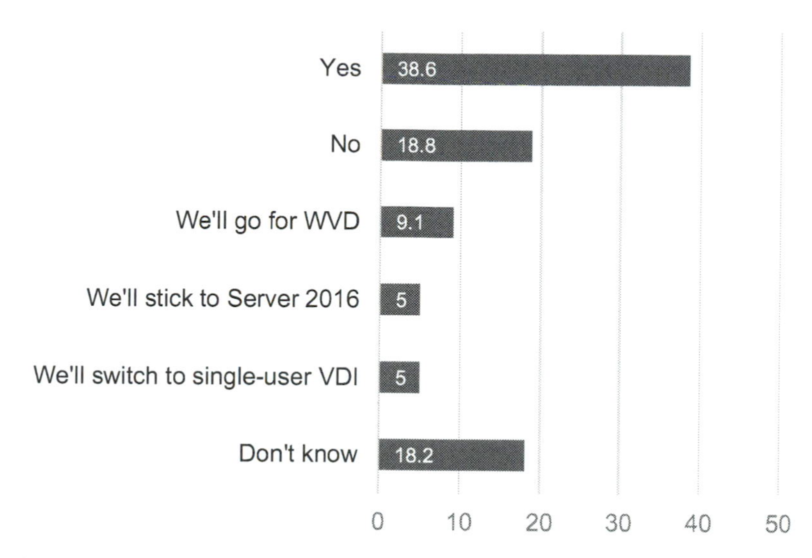


**Q: Where are your applications and data located? Or most anyway.**

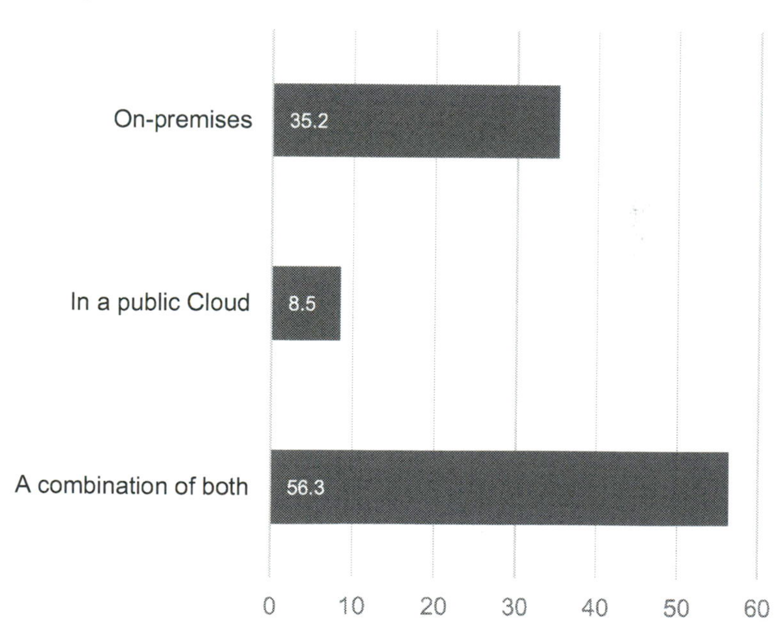

**"We believe we're moving out of the Ice Age, the Iron Age, the Industrial Age, the Information Age, to the participation age. You get on the Net and you do stuff. You IM (instant-message), you blog, you take pictures, you publish, you podcast, you transact, you distance-learn, you telemedicine. You are participating on the Internet, not just viewing stuff. We build the infrastructure that goes in the datacenter that facilitates the participation age. We build that big friggin' Webtone switch. It has security, directory, identity, privacy, storage, compute, the whole Web services stack."** – Scott McNealy

**Q: The use of SaaS only is a utopia for most enterprises worldwide.**

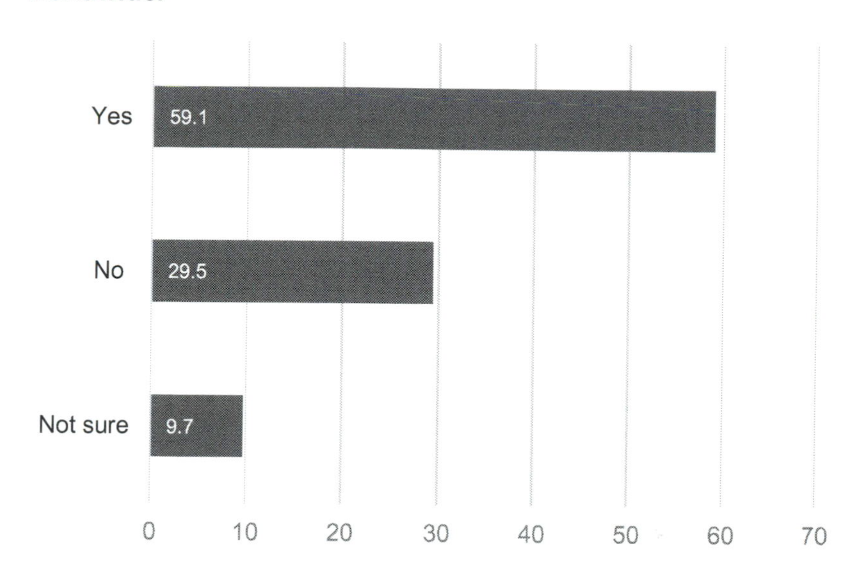


**Q: Are you considering Desktop-as-a-Service (DaaS) anytime soon?**

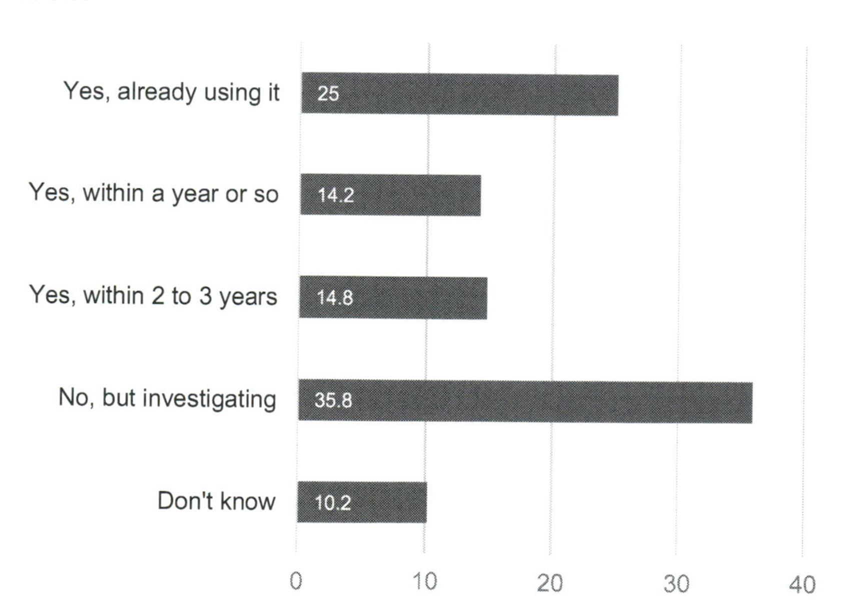

**Q: Having a Cloud-first strategy and/or vision for 2020/2025 should be a top priority.**

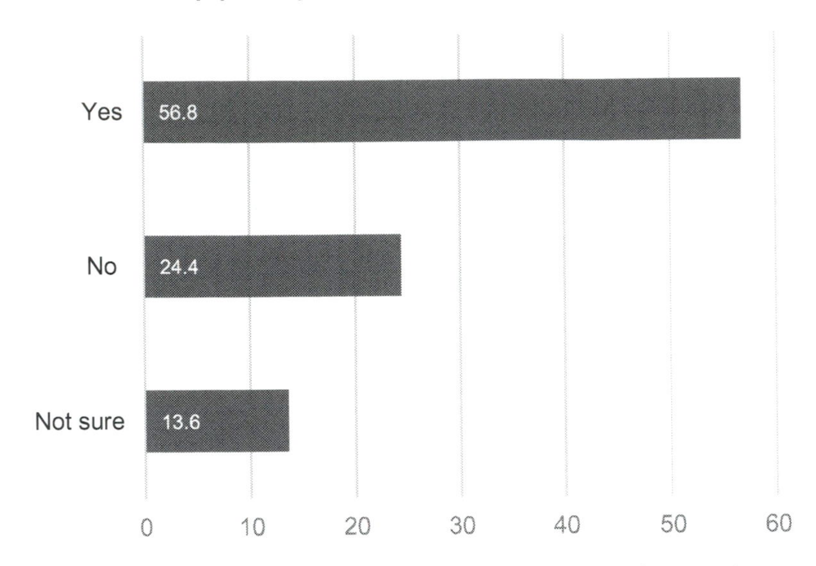


**Q: The next Cloud war will be fought in our own datacenters. Meaning hybrid Cloud is the only true way forward.**

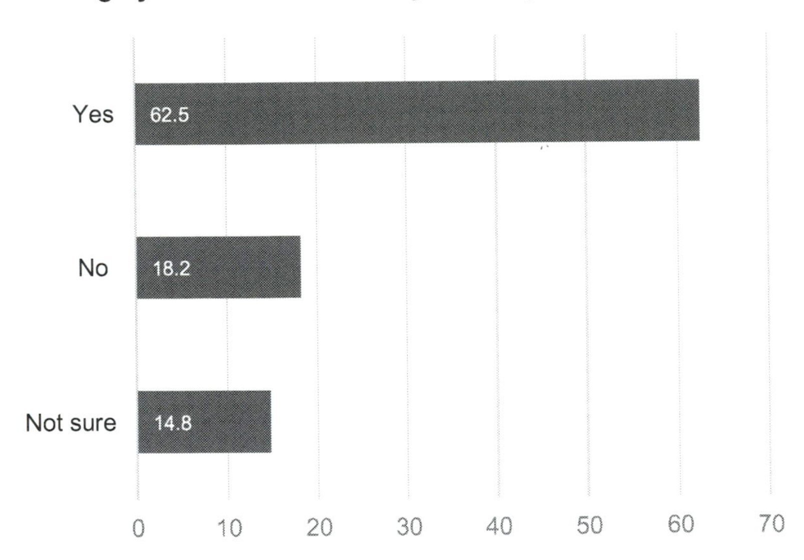

**Q: If cost savings are one of your primary drivers to consider in adopting Cloud technologies, you should rethink your game plan.**

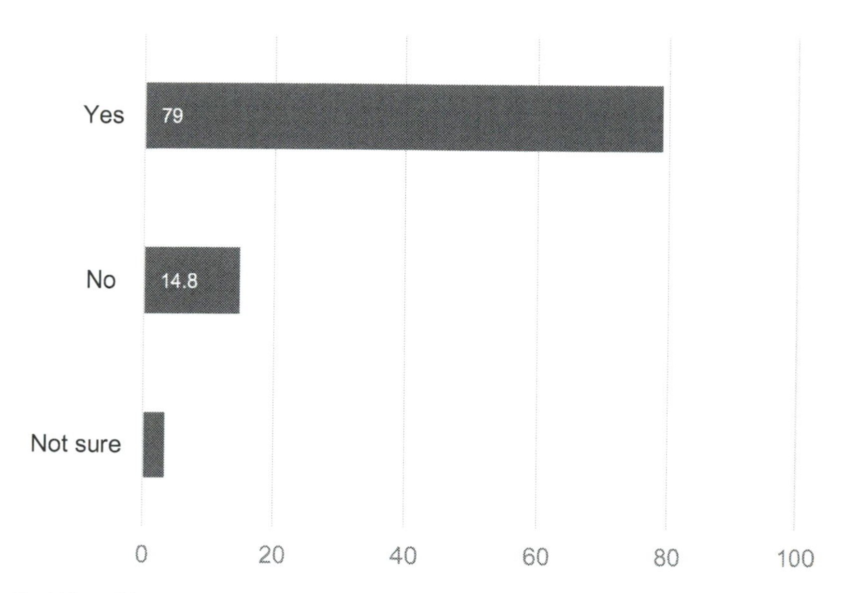


**Q: 5G will be a game-changer for everything Cloud-related.**

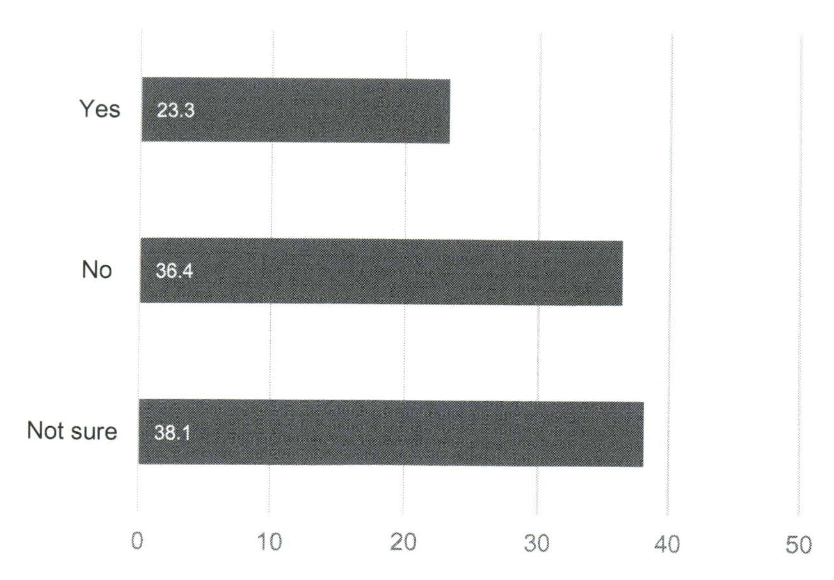

**Q: Who will be the biggest Cloud vendor within five years?**

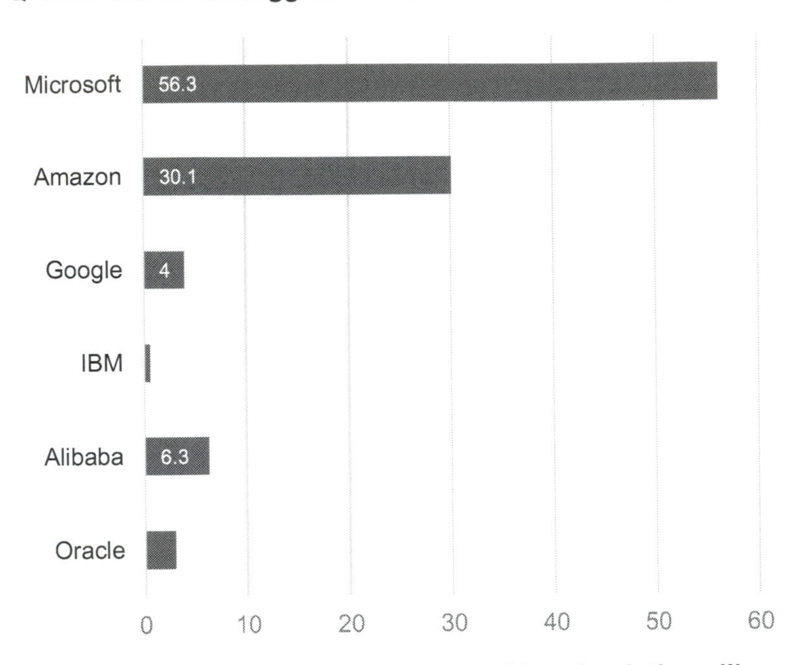


**Q: There is still too much focus on traditional solutions like VDI and SBC. They're being kept 'alive' solely for revenue purposes.**

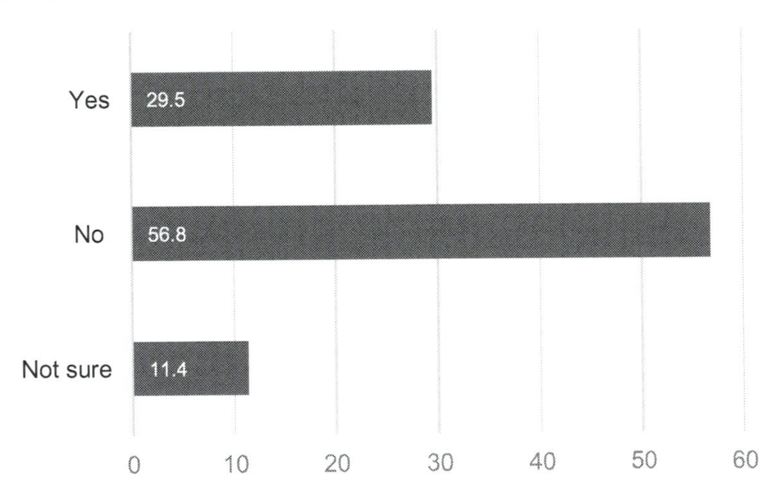

**Q: Lift and shift to the Cloud is a bad idea, period.**

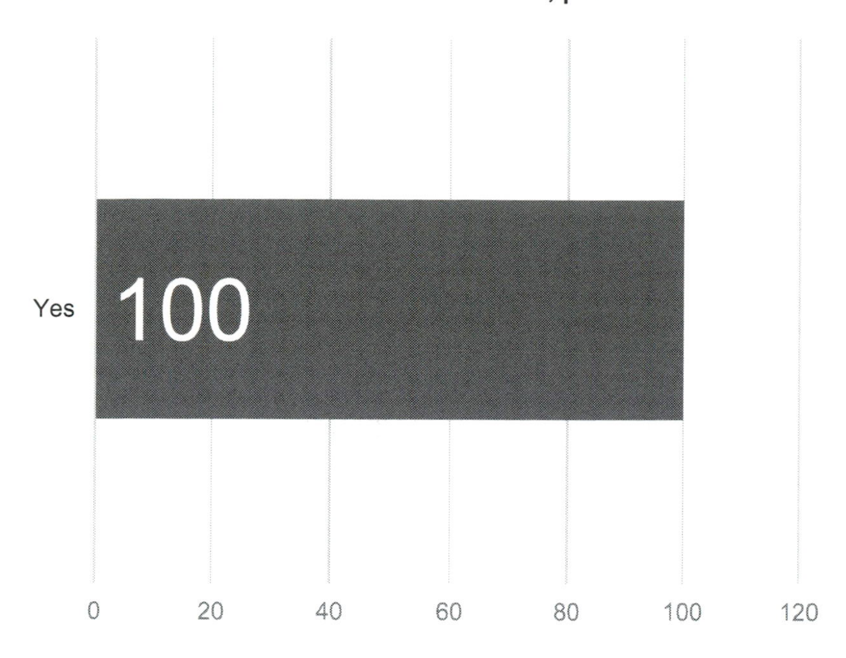


**"If you suck now, you'll be pleasantly surprised by the lack of change when you move to the Cloud."**

– Chris Hoff

## The 'Others'

### Q: Once released, the Microsoft Windows Virtual Desktop #WVD will have a major impact on DaaS going forward

1. I strongly believe in web apps. Not sure how that fits with DaaS.
2. No need for DaaS.
3. Very much depends at the moment, early impressions not brilliant.

### Q: Is 2019 the year of VDI/DaaS?

1. It's a stepping stone to the next wave.
2. Haven't they all been recently!?
3. I do not think any year is the "year of VDI/DaaS". I believe that the adoption rate of VDI/DaaS will simply increase each year, but I do not expect a big bang.
4. Have you've been living under a rock the past decade?
5. Maybe.

### Q: 'Cloud only' can become a reality within 10 to 15 years

1. For some companies for sure. For larger enterprises this may never happen and if yes, it will potentially take more than 10-15 years.
2. For some enterprises.
3. For some (small) orgs: sure! For others definitely not.
4. Who knows? – 10 to 15 years is quite far away in our industry
5. Shorter time than that.
6. Depends on business size, age, etc. and how much legacy baggage they carry.
7. Sooner, I reckon 5 to 10 years.
8. Cloud will only succeed at this when privacy and compliancy are properly taken care of.

**Q: There's too much focus on Cloud-based workspaces and other EUC-related services. The true power (and future) of 'the Cloud' lies within other technologies and developments like BIG data, AI, VR and more**

1. It's again a stepping stone.
2. In a couple of years those other technologies will have the main focus.
3. There is not a definitive future for Cloud. It will be all the current offerings (and more).
4. No. True power is out there. Just as I previously stated.
5. Both are important services and will be pushed.
6. UEM, AI, ML, Zerotrust, AR, app store distribution model.
7. Neither.
8. Moving workloads to Cloud 1st tech, a hybrid answer to Yes ;-)

**Q: Latency, poor network configurations, and statured connections in general are some of the biggest threats to successful Cloud adoption**

1. Adoption is not dependent on configuration. It lies within inspiring the users to really use the platforms' capabilities.
2. No it's the data+on prem dc.
3. As well as underestimating costs.
4. No, stupid concepts are.
5. SD-WAN is the solution.
6. No, security and control are.
7. In our case, "Algeria". Yes.
8. Security and privacy.
9. Security.

**Q: Do you think that the next Windows Server 202.x version will include the Remote Desktop Services (RDSH) roles?**

1. We don't wait. We'll go for Windows Virtual Desktop.

2. Host? No. Gateway/broker? Maybe (thinking Azure, though).
3. Not relevant (only use W10).
4. In case WVD is not available on-prem (which so far it isn't) I hope the RDSH role will still be available for a while.
5. You know how I feel about SBC/VDI.
6. Whatever happened to webification of apps?
7. Don't care. Linux ftw.
8. No need for RDSH.
9. Microsoft would sincerely like to but a lot depends on success of alternative options (WVD/Server Mgmt.).

**Q: The use of SaaS only is a utopia for most enterprises worldwide.**

1. Yes. But in a further future it could/should work.
2. Good for some, expensive for many smaller businesses who need the same tools.
3. That is how it should be delivered to the organization. Maybe in Private Cloud or Public.

**Q: Having a Cloud-first strategy and/or vision for 2020/2025 should be a top priority**

1. Cloud first is no strategy / vision.
2. Depends on the business case.
3. Depends on circumstances – has to be done right or can be very expensive.
4. Organizations tend to look at costs vs. benefit. A "Cloud-first strategy" cannot be a goal in itself. For enterprises, the Cloud is simply a means to achieve something.
5. Hybrid.
6. Cloud is a means to an end, not a goal!
7. Certainly high on the agenda.
8. Having a clear strategy and choosing the right solution should be top priority.

9. Not really. I guess most the people like to have a hybrid Cloud strategy due to loads of security, compliance and control reasons.

**Q: The next Cloud war will be fought in our own datacenters. Meaning hybrid Cloud is the only true way forward.**

1. Never going to happen... the matrix is near... One big datacenter shared in our brains hooked up to the mainframe!
2. It depends.
3. No, the Cloud war will be between those enterprises that can actually offer full Cloud solutions: Microsoft, Google, Amazon and a few others such as IBM and Oracle.
4. Different for each type of enterprise. Most government agencies will never go Cloud only.
5. The truth is out there.
6. The truth is much more diverse than this.
7. Depends on what public Cloud providers are going to do.
8. Success for Cloud vendors is all about API/integration imho, forget silos, winners should believe in their products first.

**Q: If cost savings are one of your primary drivers to consider in adopting Cloud technologies, you should rethink your game plan**

1. IT spending will not go down in the next 10 years, focus on value rather than costs.
2. Near future, yes. Distant future, no.
3. Depending on the size of the organization.
4. My answer is no w/caveat. Vendors need to get real w/ true cost of Cloud in the short term.

**Q: 5G will be a game-changer for everything Cloud-related.**

5. Could be ;)
6. 4G and fiber optics should be sufficient if the backend is properly designed and configured.
7. It will be a catalyst.
8. Depends on what the Chinese want with it.

**Q: Who will be the biggest Cloud vendor within five years?**

1. The one who is selling beers!
2. Don't know.
3. It's a Hybrid world and only 1x vendor will be ahead for a period of time. It's all about h/w cycles in the backend vs. front stuff we consume. No one is the center.
4. The aliens who control the mind of Elon Musk.
5. No idea, so many unknown factors.

**Q: There is still too much focus on traditional solutions like VDI and SBC. They're being kept 'alive' solely for revenue purposes**

1. Kept alive because of legacy apps, allow organizations not to upgrade their apps, and keep legacy software builders remain client/server-based.
2. As long as there are traditional apps, there will be something like VDI and/or SBC.
3. I asked my wife what this means and she said: "How would I know?" There's that for relevance.
4. Suspicion from myself that this is a generational dependency: next gen workforce will not care about having a desktop session. They will already have it, their own device, apps/services, delivered straight to it!

**Sponsored content**

*'To measure is to know, to guess is to miss, and knowledge is power'*: that is the adage of SALOMON.

SALOMON provides organizations with insights into whether their organization makes effective use of existing IT resources and applications and outlines various scenarios on how companies can effectively change and optimize. SALOMON analyzes your IT infrastructure and business processes from the perspective of the end-user experience and management at the same time.

***"We specialize in various assessments (security, technical, business) and help companies of all sizes to get a grip on what it is they need to do to stay competitive."***

Since Salomon is fully independent and unbiased in every way, we often get asked to review technical as well as functional designs proposed by other third-party companies. This way our customers know for sure that they won't run into any surprises afterwards, financially or otherwise. A second opinion, if you will.

If needed, and it often is, Salomon provides detailed roadmaps outlining in detail what it is our customers need to do going forward, from a technical as well as a business perspective. These can be short- or long-term engagements where we fully embrace the customers' mission statements, future plans and/or wishes.

Contact us at info@salomon-it.nl or call +31 (0)6 11 58 33 23

## Q: Lift and shift to the Cloud is a bad idea, period

When we posted the survey we mentioned that we wanted to have a bit of fun as well. This question is a good example of that. The only answer possible was 'Yes'. In general almost everyone agrees, though there were some who replied or sent me (Bas) a personal message with a short explanation why multiple answers would have been appropriate, or an 'Other' option. Fair enough, of course. Even though the option wasn't there, there were a couple of *other* remarks that came with this specific question. They all thought it was funny, by the way.

1. Lift and shift does happen, and there are some good use cases where it does work. Personally I have had some good experiences with this approach. It's not as black and white as most people think.
2. According to Microsoft's Datacenter Migration for MSP Best Practices, this is the way to go. Lift and shift, adjust later. Cost-wise, this may have a negative impact; however, adjusting your strategy also slows down the adoption of services like AI and others, for example.
3. Back in 2007 I did the ultimate lift and shift. We had to 'lift' a physical machine from abroad. I had a colleague coming with a PowerEdge machine as hand luggage, literally under his arm. Everything was well prepared and we were able to mount it in our datacenter. Total downtime was around 4.5 hours. It was an Exchange server behind a slow WAN link. We had to come up with something, right?
4. For a lot of companies it's often the first step into Cloud computing.

# Appendices

# Appendix A – Cloud "quotes"

In order of appearance…

"If you can't explain it simply, you don't understand it well enough." – Albert Einstein

"Public speaking is like learning to drive and shifting gears in a car. When you know your content, it all goes automatically with adrenaline as engine fuel!" – Christiaan Brinkhoff

"Do what you love, and you'll never work another day in your life." – Marc Anthony

"To empower the children of developing countries to learn by providing one connected laptop to every school-age child." – OLPC

"If you've started with the technology, you've already lost focus of your business requirements and made the assumption that your business needs to fit the technology." – Chris Marks

"Cloud is about how you do computing, not where you do computing." – Paul Maritz

"There's no way that company exists in a year." – Tom Siebel

"Running Any App on Any Device by Any User is great, but just because you can run AutoCAD on your smartphone, doesn't mean you should." – Johan van Amersfoort

"Above all, make sure that you have documented things well enough so that you and your customer, if there is one, can fully understand the process without having to reconstruct major parts of it. Don't forget the backup and disaster recovery aspects, which do not always get as much attention as they should!" – Tobias Kreidl

"Some of the established vendors try to (duct tape) transform their 'born in on-premises era' product and deliver this as a service in the public Cloud, while others design and build solutions with public Cloud services as the starting point." – Ruben Spruijt

"I don't need a hard disk in my computer if I can get to the server faster... carrying around these non-connected computers is Byzantine by comparison." – Steve Jobs

"Before you start with your Cloud strategy, you should already have an exit strategy." – Kees Baggerman

"We all have had production machines that just can't die for some reason, so why not use a cut-over or maintenance window to change the way they're accessed as well?" – Adam Yarborough

"It is important to store as much data as possible in appropriate short intervals. Even if there is no business case currently, no marketing approach, or if a certain sensor seems to be unimportant." – Marcel Meurer

"The mediocre teacher tells. The good teacher explains. The superior teacher demonstrates. The great teacher inspires."
– William Arthur Ward

"The computer industry is the only industry that is more fashion-driven than women's fashion. Maybe I'm an idiot, but I have no idea what anyone is talking about. What is it? It's complete gibberish. It's insane. When is this idiocy going to stop? We'll make Cloud computing announcements. I'm not going to fight this thing. But I don't understand what we would do differently in the light of Cloud." – Larry Ellison

"In most cases, research tells us that this is not yet possible for the customer in question. This has mainly to do with necessary 'legacy' applications that are not available as an SaaS service or can be moved to the Cloud." – Robin Hobo

"Mobile phones are misnamed. They should be called gateways to human knowledge." – Ray Kurzweil

"The nature of the Cloud makes VM-instances and -pricing fluctuating. New VM-instances are introduced regularly and are influencing pricing, so what is not feasible today may be a real possibility tomorrow." – Rasmus Raun-Nielsen

"Every other vendor after your strategic one should be able to implement with the first. That's how you build the best possible ecosystem for your IT, that's how you build a successful Cloud journey, that's how you build a great experience for you as an admin." – Simon Binder

"Businesses are consuming SaaS applications more than before, and having a solid Cloud-federated identity model has never been as important." – Brian Timp

"There were 5 exabytes of information created between the dawn of civilization through 2003, but that much information is now created every day." – Eric Schmidt

"You don't know what you don't know." – Socrates

"The guy who knows about computers is the last person you want to have creating documentation for people who don't understand computers." – Adam Osborne

"Virtual Reality was once the dream of science fiction. But the Internet was also once a dream and so were computers and smartphones." – Mark Zuckerberg

"In the event of nuclear war, the only things to survive will be cockroaches, Twinkies, and Windows apps." – Shawn Bass

"Remember – a change of premises does not solve problems. If you aren't managing resources well in your datacenter, the problems only get worse in the Cloud." – DJ Eshelman

"Line-of-business leaders everywhere are bypassing IT departments to get applications from the Cloud (also known as Software-as-a-Service, or SaaS) and paying for them like they would a magazine subscription. And when the service is no longer required, they can cancel that subscription with no equipment left unused in the corner." – Daryl Plummer

"DOS is fundamental for Windows, and Windows will be the fundament for Microsoft Azure." – This quote reminds me of how fast we are going (and some of you already did) to leverage Azure Cloud Platform Services." – Christiaan Brinkhoff

"Anything else is just a service tied to manual labor, which is not Cloud-centric and will fail due to introduced irregularities as well as unsurmountable labor efforts." – Mitch Meade

"Monitor VMs utilization on the Cloud constantly to make sure that all resources are being utilized efficiently as using a pay-as-you-go model means you are charged for the VM size/option regardless of how much CPU/memory is being used within." – Saadallah Chebaro

"When you have a Cloud-only strategy and don't re platform your workloads, you are preparing to fail as the cost will be massive. Only use the Cloud when it's the correct platform for your workloads or you are architect using Cloud services." – Ronnie Hamilton

"The lift-and-shift scenario makes the Cloud an expensive new hosting solution for your servers, without providing you a lot of new possibilities." – Marcel Kornegoor

"If you don't jump on the new, you don't survive." – Satya Nadella

"Virtual Machines in the Cloud are the worst of both worlds, don't do it." – Jim Moyle

"The last ten years of IT have been about changing the way people work. The next ten years of it will be about transforming your business." – Aaron Levie

"The time taken for a packet to be transferred across a network. You can measure this as one way to its destination or as a round trip." – Latency

"The factory of the future will have only two employees, a man, and a dog. The man will be there to feed the dog. The dog will be there to keep the man from touching the equipment." – Alice Kahn

"Regardless of the situation, first determine your technical requirements and then find tools that meet those requirements now and in the foreseeable future." – Ned Bellavance

"When consuming virtual machines from an IaaS provider, use automation or power plans to pause or shutdown virtual machines whenever they don't have to be used to reduce cost." – Ivan de Mes

"Doing off premise is like shitting while away from home. Never feels as good as on premise." – Cláudio Rodrigues

"We became much more data-driven – gathering insight from one-on-one meetings with customers and partners and targeted questionnaires to our vast customer base using virtualization today." – Scott Manchester

"Moving to Office 365 will not negate the need for storage locally (I know some will be shocked by this), you'll still need storage on local devices for caching data (i.e. OneDrive, Outlook OST)." – David Wilkinson

"By using some conservative calculations in Azure calculator, the total cost of storage can drop anywhere between 20% and 40%, based on Azure Files consumption and original size of the system disk. Azure Files brings a list of benefits to the table." – Stefan Georgiev

"To all users of technology who are willing to take a chance, make a choice, and try a new way of doing things so that we can nurture and enjoy a happy, healthy planet." – Katherine Murray

"Whenever possible try to leverage purpose-built Cloud services for your use case." – René Bigler

"A good rule of IT is the more canaries (layers) in the coal mine, the better it will be for you and your users. If you can detect problems with a small percentage of users vs. all the users being impacted, that is a good day." – Patrick Coble

"If you have built castles in the air, your work need not be lost; that is where they should be. Now put the foundations under them."
– Henry David Thoreau

"To prevent cryptojacking attacks, make sure that your Cloud instances are as secure as your on-premises ones and follow all the security best practices – strong passwords, multi-factor authentication, monitor utilization of servers (and processes) and keep an eye on all security news." – Martin Zugec

"CASB provides security on SaaS on an API level and which allows it to be able to look at end-user activity and determine if certain activities are abnormal or not." – Marius Sandbu

"Unlike a drop of water which loses its identity when it joins the ocean, man does not lose his being in the society in which he lives. Man's life is independent. He is born not for the development of the society alone, but for the development of his self."
– B. R. Ambedkar

"I cannot highly recommend the book: *The Phoenix Project: A Novel About IT, DevOps, and Helping Your Business Win*. Organizations failing to do so will fall behind their competition or even worse, go completely out of business. I would even go so far as demanding all my employees read it and an exam to verify."
– Trond E. Haavarstein

"Be the Automator, not the Automated." – Trond E. Haavarstein

“Is that person worth 4 times the number of reboots and 10 times the number of security patches? The answer might be yes, or the answer might be, as Don points out, that these are IT professionals. Pro-fess-io-nals. That means you pay them money. Professionals who know how to do a job professionally. So in the IT profession, we learn new things. If you didn’t want to learn new things, you should get into lumber. There has not been a new tree in quite a long time.” – Jeffrey Snover

“The first rule of any technology used in a business is that automation applied to an efficient operation will magnify the efficiency. The second is that automation applied to an inefficient operation will magnify the inefficiency.” – Bill Gates

“Release a desktop that just works as quickly as possible to your users and see the response from your users as positive (continuous) feedback. And put this feedback on a prioritized list (product backlog). This way you know what the users (customers) want/need the most in the desktop.” – Chris Twiest

“Any roles involved in a project that do not directly contribute toward the goal of putting valuable software in the hands of users as quickly as possible should be carefully considered.”
– Stein Inge Morisbak

“Currently, DevOps is more like a philosophical movement, not yet a precise collection of practices, descriptive or prescriptive.”
– Gene Kim

“Thirty-nine years of my life had passed before I understood that Clouds were not my enemy; that they were beautiful, and that I needed them. I suppose this, for me, marked the beginning of wisdom. Life is short.” – Imani David

"Creating a movie starts with a script. Building houses starts with a plan. So should your journey to the Cloud." – Bart Jacobs

"Everything is going to be connected to Cloud and data... All of this will be mediated by software." – Satya Nadella

"Consider where your users are based and ensure that the region being used to host your infrastructure is in the same location. Test connectivity, ensure that there is not a high amount of latency between your end-users and the target platform." – Leee Jeffries

"Imagine a world where everything that can be connected will be connected – where driverless cars talk to smart transportation networks and where wireless sensors can monitor your health and transmit data to your doctor. That's a snapshot of what the 5G world will look like." – Ajit Pai

"Cloud is just somebody else's datacenter" – Patrick van den Born and Anton van Pelt

"If costs savings is your primary driver to consider, or adopt 'Cloud' you should rethink your game plan." – Bas van Kaam

"The Biggest Benefit of Cloud Computing is Lowering Costs."
– John Doe

"Besides using different platform services in the Cloud, always make use of reserved instances and power management tooling when leveraging IaaS Cloud infrastructures to make it more affordable for your business – when lift and shift is the only option."
– Christiaan Brinkhoff

"So many times have I seen companies struggle down the line when poor investment is made into the basic design and layout of their Cloud presence, be that fully Cloud-driven or hybrid. Start with the basics, region, network, storage, access and work your way up to the Virtual Machines." – Dave Brett

"It won't be cheap if you plan on using the exact same amount of resources you would in the office building. What you want is to make use of all the smart features Cloud elasticity offers." – Sander Noordijk

"But when you actually look at the cost per hour, per desktop, and then multiply that by all the hours you need those desktops to run, the Cloud can get really expensive!" – Brian Madden

"You can offer your product in a more flexible way, so you might make it available for people who would otherwise not use your product at all. Sometimes you don't need to buy a car, you just want to go to the movies." – Dennis Smith

"It has been proven that modernization and moving towards PaaS will lower the operational costs significantly. The second advantage in this process is that when the next evolution / migration of infrastructure comes along... for example, say a "microservices type architecture", they will then be able to move to that type of infrastructure much easier." – Adnan Hendricks

"You don't want to find out during a disaster/failover that you missed/forgot a component." – Adin Ermie

"You can have data without information, but you cannot have information without data." – Daniel Keys Moran

KEEP CALM AND ALWAYS ASK WHY – Anonymous

“It wasn’t raining when Noah built the Ark.” – Howard Ruff

“Without data you’re just another person with an opinion, especially in a Cloud environment.” – Eltjo van Gulik & Ryan Ververs-Bijkerk

“Never trust a computer you can’t throw out a window.” – Unknown

“Never let a computer know you’re in a hurry.” – Jeff Pesis

“In SLA management, you think services, see SLA, hear SLO, perform SLA management.” – Mussadiq Abdul Rahim

“If you think you’ve seen this movie before, you are right. Cloud computing is based on the time-sharing model we leveraged years ago before we could afford our own computers. The idea is to share computing power among many companies and people, thereby reducing the cost of that computing power to those who leverage it. The value of time share and the core value of Cloud computing are pretty much the same, only the resources these days are much better and more cost-effective.” – David Linthicum

“There was a time when every household, town, farm or village had its own water well. Today, shared public utilities give us access to clean water by simply turning on the tap; Cloud computing works in a similar fashion. Just like water from the tap in your kitchen, Cloud computing services can be turned on or off quickly as needed. Like at the water company, there is a team of dedicated professionals making sure the service provided is safe, secure and available on a 24/7 basis. When the tap isn’t on, not only are you saving water, but you aren’t paying for resources you don’t currently need.”
– Vivek Kundra

“The Value of your IT Investments is only as Big as you Train your Users (users includes IT Staff).” – Jasper Kraak

"Education is the passport to the future, for tomorrow belongs to those who prepare for it today." – Malcolm X

"Share what you know when you can, but what I think matters most is to share your questions, ideas and opinions. It will enrich all of us." – James Ma

"Lack of education, the problem is." – Yoda

"In over your head? Make sure to carve the subject up into smaller sections or steps. That way you won't lose focus." – Sander Bruijs

"Cloud computing is actually a spectrum of things complementing one another and building on a foundation of sharing. Inherent dualities in the Cloud computing phenomenon are spawning divergent strategies for Cloud computing success. The public Cloud, hybrid Clouds, and private Clouds now dot the landscape of IT-based solutions. Because of that, the basic issues have moved from 'what is Cloud? to 'how will Cloud projects evolve?" – Chris Howard

"After all, our main goal as EUC consultants is to deliver the right solution for the job. This means giving a hammer to someone that is using nails and not a screwdriver. Keep that in mind at all times. Right tool for the job. Always." – Cláudio Rodrigues

"In computer networking, a failure domain encompasses a section of a network that is negatively affected when a critical device or network service experiences problems. The size of a failure domain and its potential impact depends on the device or service that is malfunctioning. For example, a router potentially experiencing problems would generally create a more significant failure domain than a network switch would. Smaller failure domains reduce the risk of disruption over a large section of a network, and ease the troubleshooting process." – Wikipedia

"Mobile use is growing faster than all of Google's internal predictions." – Eric Schmidt

"We believe we're moving out of the Ice Age, the Iron Age, the Industrial Age, the Information Age, to the participation age. You get on the Net and you do stuff. You IM (instant-message), you blog, you take pictures, you publish, you podcast, you transact, you distance-learn, you telemedicine. You are participating on the Internet, not just viewing stuff. We build the infrastructure that goes in the datacenter that facilitates the participation age. We build that big friggin' Webtone switch. It has security, directory, identity, privacy, storage, compute, the whole Web services stack." – Scott McNealy